# Hiking Lake Louise

*Walking, hiking, backpacking, and off-trail scrambling in the Lake Louise area*

# Mike Potter

LUMINOUS
COMPOSITIONS

**IMPORTANT SAFETY NOTE: Those who participate in the activities described in this guidebook must be prepared for risks and must know how to evaluate them in order to proceed safely.** See the Safety section, pages 19-26.

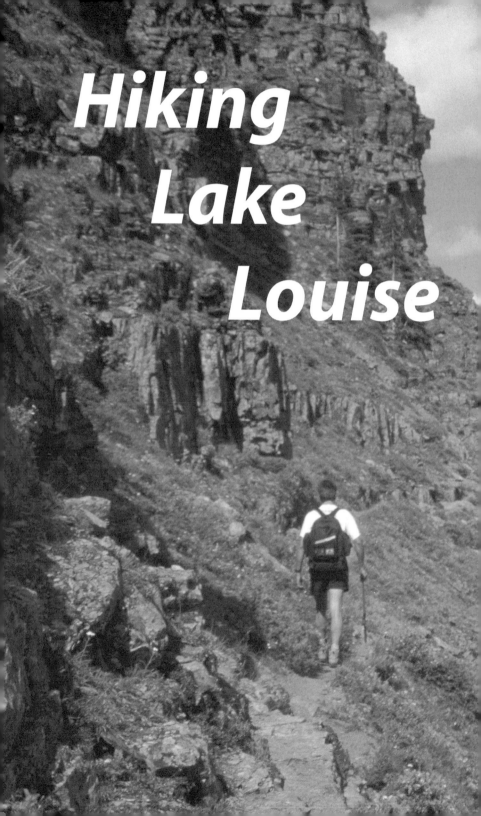

# *Hiking*

# *Lake*

# *Louise*

*Mike Potter*

*Published by*
**Luminous Compositions**
**2815 Lionel Crescent SW**
**Calgary, Alberta**
**Canada T3E 6B1**

**luminouscompositions@shaw.ca**
**www.luminouscompositions.com**


**Canadian Cataloguing in Publication Data**

Potter, Mike, 1954-
  Hiking Lake Louise

Includes index.
ISBN 0-9694438-2-X

1. Trails—Alberta—Louise, Lake, Region—Guide-books.
2. Hiking—Alberta—Louise, Lake, Region—Guide-books.
3. Backpacking—Alberta—Louise, Lake, Region—Guide-books.
4. Louise, Lake, Region (Alta.)—Guide-books.
I. Title
GV199.44.C22L346 1994          917.123'32          C94-910139-7


Printed and bound in Canada by
Friesens Corporation Book Division, Altona, Manitoba, Canada R0G 0B0
www.friesens.com

All photographs by Mike Potter.
Front and back covers: Split image of hikers on the *Lake Louise Lakeshore* trail, with view ahead to Mt. Victoria (right) and Mt. Lefroy (left).
Title (pages 2 and 3): Hiker returning from off-trail scramble of Devils Thumb.
Contents (p. 8): The pinnacle known as the Tooth, east above Sentinel Pass on the off-trail scrambling route up Mt. Temple, with upper part of Paradise Valley below.

4

# Foreword to Original Edition

Mike Potter appeared at the park-naturalist office in Jasper one day, wanting to volunteer his services. Aha! I thought; this guy is *keen*. He was in town all winter, writing natural-history items for the local newspaper, preparing evening programs, making himself indispensable. But we lost him that spring, when the parks service offered him a proper park-interpreter's position at Lake Louise.

Mike is that rarity: a park employee genuinely fascinated with the park; a park naturalist who really *likes* to naturalize. During his summers at Lake Louise, Mike walked, scrambled and boulder-hopped every bit of the area that didn't demand a rope. It shows in this guidebook; in reading it, you *know* he has been there, taking careful notes at every trail junction.

It was a pleasure editing Mike's Lake Louise hiking guide. Reading it reminded me of soul-filling days spent high above the certified Gem of the Rockies — memories of the Saddleback at the height of fall color, of the Big Beehive in a walloping thunderstorm, of flowery ledges along the Plain of Six Glaciers trail.

Read this book on a Thursday evening. Turn off the television and read this book. Pick out a trail — any trail around Lake Louise; they're all great — and let the promise of a day stumping up and down in the mountains get you through Friday's folly. On Saturday, take Mike's book with you. Jam it in your pack pocket over and over as the weekends go by, until it's dog-eared and dirty and much-loved. Write in it. ("July 22nd. Did the Larch Valley — Paradise Valley loop. Saw a wolverine!") ("August 18th. Wenkchemna Pass, finally. Snowed. Golden eagle flew by so close I could have touched it.")

This guide is a fine piece of work, and that's not surprising: there's a bit of Mike Potter on every page.

— Ben Gadd, January 21, 1990

**View southeast from *The Plain of Six Glaciers* trail over the moraines of the Lower Victoria Glacier and to (l to r) Fairview Mountain, Haddo Peak, and Mt. Aberdeen.**

# Acknowledgements for 2005 Edition

I am grateful to the many people who gave me assistance with this book.

Special thanks go to John Blum, then of Woodruff & Blum Booksellers in Lake Louise, who suggested the need for this book and who gave welcome encouragement during its genesis. His material contribution is much appreciated.

Ben Gadd of Jasper, author and publisher of the highly successful **Handbook of the Canadian Rockies**, was the thorough and very knowledgeable editor of the original edition. Ben graciously wrote the foreword in his inimitable, entertaining style.

Michael Luski, then coordinator in the Writing and Publishing program at The Banff Centre, opened my eyes to many aspects of the publishing business and offered much insightful and practical advice.

Cyndi Smith of Coyote Books and Walter Lanz of Oak House Publishing generously shared their hard-earned expertise in self-publishing.

Perry Davis of Banff National Park gave enthusiastic support and a valued review of the trails information. Jeff Waugh of the park gave a helpful review of the interpretive information. Heather Dempsey, also of the park, gave valued comments and answered or clarified numerous points.

Other Banff National Park staff who contributed to this guide include: Rob Harding, Jim Mulchinock, Kim Fraser, Tim Auger, Pierce Achtymichuk, Mike Kerr, Alex Kolesch, Anders Hawkins, and Roger Hostin.

The late Jon Whyte, then Curator of the Heritage Collection at the Whyte Museum of the Canadian Rockies, Banff, gave me help with some questions of history and geography. Mary Andrews, Lena Goon, and Alex Huculak of the Archives, Whyte Museum of the Canadian Rockies, were of great assistance in my research.

Staff at the **Banff Crag & Canyon** encouraged my column *Backcountry Banff*, out of which this guidebook developed. I thank in particular Stewart Muir, editor when I first proposed my column; subsequent editor Richard Blonski; and Bob Doull, then President, Black Tusk Newspapers.

Donna Nelson of Gem Trek Publishing clarified many points regarding trail distances, and trail and peak elevations.

Jim Beckel of Friesens' Calgary office was ever-helpful, and Brad Schmidt of Technical Support at Friesens' Altona plant was patient and professional regarding my many requests for assistance in working with new computer hardware and software.

My wife Jane gave essential support and encouragement, particularly with her excellent proofreading skills.


Any errors in this book are my responsibility; if you spot any, please write to me at 2815 Lionel Crescent SW, Calgary, Alberta, Canada T3E 6B1, or send an e-mail to: luminouscompositions@shaw.ca

# Preface to the 2005 revised edition

This is the fourth edition of **Hiking Lake Louise**, the first of my seven titles to date on the Rockies, the one that got me started as a book author and publisher fifteen years ago.

This 2005 edition incorporates changes since the 1999 edition, maintaining the accuracy of the descriptions. The section of colour photos added in the second edition remains, giving an enhanced impression of the vivid surroundings and fascinating wildlife of the Lake Louise area.

Details on the eight other books currently available from Luminous Compositions can be obtained by e-mail, by post, or on the website (addresses on p. 4).

Briefly, the other Luminous titles are: **Backcountry Banff**, companion to this book, covering all the rest of Banff National Park; **Ridgewalks in the Canadian Rockies**, describing over 140 outings to panoramic ridges; **Fire Lookout Hikes in the Canadian Rockies**, highlighting 82 hikes in Alberta and B.C. with great views and fascinating history; **White Wilderness: The Canadian Rockies in Winter**, a photographic portfolio of the snowy season; **Central Rockies Wildflowers**, a compact identification guide to over 115 species; **Central Rockies Placenames**, giving the story of over 1000 placenames; **Central Rockies Mammals** by John Marriott, with lively accounts and superb photos of 38 species; and **Columbia Valley Guide** by Denise Lemaster, a comprehensive reference to the area from Radium Hot Springs to Canal Flats in B.C.

Hope you enjoy the Lake Louise area. Take good care of it, too: stewardship is the best way to ensure that this area will retain its wild character.

Mike Potter
February, 2005

**The author on the *Upper Victoria Glacier Access* trail, with views of (l to r) Mitre Peak, Mt. Lefroy, Abbot Pass and The Deathtrap, and Mt. Victoria.**

# Contents

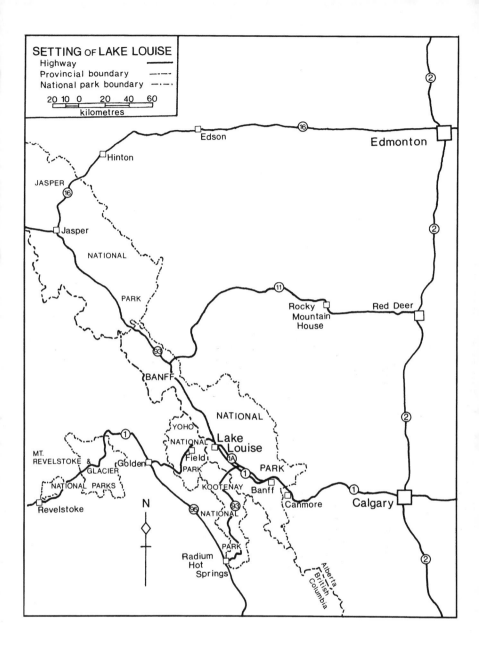

SETTING OF LAKE LOUISE
Highway
Provincial boundary
National park boundary

20 10 0  20  40  60
kilometres

# Introduction

The body of water that the Stoney people know as Ho-run-num-nay, the "Lake of the Little Fishes," lies in a valley close to some of the higher peaks in the Canadian Rockies. The first non-Native to behold Lake Louise was Tom Wilson, who—led by a Stoney guide—reached its eastern shore in 1882.

The completion in 1885 of a transcontinental line on the Canadian Pacific Railway route, along with the construction in 1890 of the first commercial accommodation at Lake Louise, attracted increasing numbers of visitors. The Lake Louise area became an international destination, largely due to promotion by the CPR.

Pioneers such as Walter Wilcox and Samuel Allen explored and mapped much of the vicinity. The surrounding mountains became a mecca for alpinists. Their activities created notoriety for the area with the first climbing fatality in North America—the death of Philip Stanley Abbot in a fall during an 1896 attempt on Mt. Lefroy—but its appeal did not diminish.

Legislation created the Lake Louise Forest Park in 1892, but it was not until ten years later that the area including Lake Louise and Moraine Lake came under the protection of an expanded Banff National Park. Recreational hikers were drawn by a proliferation of trails, such as those to Lake Agnes and the Saddleback—built in the early 1890s under the supervision of Willoughby Astley, first manager of the original chalet. A number of teahouses provided to cater to visitors proved popular (two of them, at the Plain of Six Glaciers and Lake Agnes, are still in operation).

The works of the many painters who responded to the Lake Louise area, including Belmore Browne, the Group of Seven's Lawren Harris, and Banff residents Peter and Catharine Whyte, helped to further spread recognition of the region. Road construction facilitated access, and visitors flocked to see for themselves the renowned scenery.

The Lake Louise area has become one of the premier attractions of Banff National Park, and indeed of the entire Canadian Rockies. You can marvel at the panoramic vistas from a distance, but to gain a better appreciation of these fabled environs, head out on foot to experience their fascination firsthand.

This guidebook beckons you to explore more than 250 kilometres (over 155 miles) of trails and routes in Banff National Park within a 16 km (10 mi) radius centred on Lake Louise village. This area of some 600 square kilometres, with its concentration of hiking possibilities, can be the focus of excursions—whether short walks, day hikes, backpacking trips, or off-trail scrambles—during which you will garner in-depth knowledge of natural and human history.

You will also gather what may well become some of your most cherished memories.

**N.B.** Trailheads, trail locations, and park regulations can change: ask at a park information centre for the most up-to-date information.

# Using This Guidebook

I have organized the trails and routes in the Lake Louise area into six sections, beginning with the three valleys on the west side of the Bow River—those of Lake Louise, Paradise Creek, and Moraine Lake. The short fourth section describes the trails around Lake Louise village, the fifth section the area east of Lake Louise on the opposite side of the Bow Valley, and the sixth those farther afield.

The name of each trail or route comes from its destination or its most prominent feature. If a destination can be approached two ways, the trail name indicates the direction, e.g., *Sentinel Pass from Larch Valley* or *Sentinel Pass from Paradise Valley*.

Each trail's distance is given in kilometres (km) and miles (mi), with the beginning and end points specified .

I have classified the outings, depending on their nature, as follows:

— a **walk** is short, with little (if any) elevation gain: such an outing will appeal if time is limited or if looking for an easy stroll;

— a **day hike** varies from a jaunt of a couple of hours to a full-day excursion and entails some (or considerable) elevation gain;

— a **backpack** is an overnight trip to one of the places in this book with a designated backcountry campground: Paradise Valley, Hidden Lake junction, Baker Lake, Merlin Meadows, Red Deer Lakes, Wildflower Creek, and Taylor Lake;

— an **off-trail scramble** is a route that goes off or beyond established, maintained trails. (The first edition of **Hiking Lake Louise** in 1990 was the first book to describe such options.) N.B. See the information on pages 25 and 26 of the Safety section before attempting any off-trail scramble.

Several outings are characterized as extensions of day hikes, connectors, or options. Some are on trails that may be unmaintained by Parks Canada.

The time estimate given for each trail or route is one way, based on an average pace. The estimate is for actual hiking time; extra time should be allowed for rest breaks, snacks or lunch, photography, and nature observation.

Descending a trail with lots of elevation gain clearly takes less time than the ascent; dividing the outbound estimate by two will give an idea of the time required to get down. (Do take it easy going down trails as the going can often be harder than going up due to factors like loose rocks or slippery sections. Descents can also be jarring on the knees...speaking as a recent convert, a hiking pole can be very helpful.)

The elevation gain or loss on each trail or route is given in metres (m) and feet (ft), rounded to the nearest five units except for measured points (e.g., surveyed peaks). For outings where there is a lot of up and down, the figures are cumulative totals. The maximum elevation is given in metres and feet, again usually rounded.

Trailhead info follows next: the start of each trail or route is usually a parking area, or at a specified distance along a previous description. There are trailhead kiosks (small shelters with maps and information) at the beginning of many trails.

A synopsis of each trail or route gives:

— the cumulative distance in kilometres at intermediate junctions and important features such as backcountry campgrounds;

— the elevation in metres at the beginning, significant intermediate points, and the end;

— the direction to be taken at junctions in order to reach the destination, and often where the other direction leads;

— a general description of the physical configuration of the trail (e.g., level, gradual, steep; wide, narrow; well-established, faint); and

— mention of connecting trails and routes.

The body of each description gives information on features found along the trail, such as the surrounding landscape and nearby peaks, as well as facets of natural and human history.

## Access

The Lake Louise area is readily accessible. The Trans-Canada Highway (Highway 1) passes by Lake Louise Village, which is 180 km northwest of the city of Calgary in the province of Alberta and 55 km northwest of Banff townsite. Lake Louise Village is 25 km east of the Yoho National Park community of Field, British Columbia, and 81 km east of the town of Golden, B.C.

An alternative to the Trans-Canada Highway to reach Lake Louise from Banff townsite is the Bow Valley Parkway (Hwy. 1A). The distance is only three kilometres greater at 58 km, although the time required is longer due to the slower speed limit (60 km/hr vs. 90 km/hr). This route has the attractions of being less travelled, of featuring interpretive signs at numerous pull-offs, and of offering good opportunities to sight wildlife.

Lake Louise is 233 km southeast of Jasper townsite via the spectacular Icefields Parkway (Highway 93). Lake Louise is 477 km southwest of Edmonton via Hwy. 2 almost to Red Deer, Hwy. 11A and Hwy. 11 (the David Thompson Highway) to Saskatchewan River Crossing, and the Icefields Parkway (Hwy. 93); or 460 km from Edmonton via Hwy. 2 to Olds, Hwys. 27 and 22 to Cochrane, Hwy. 1A to Morley, and the Trans-Canada Highway.

Lake Louise can be easily reached using public transportation. Frequent daily Greyhound Canada (www.greyhound.ca) buses running east and west stop at Samson Mall in Lake Louise Village. The toll-free number for schedules and fares is 1-800-661-8747. The local Lake Louise number is (403) 522-3870.

From late May to mid-October, Brewster Transportation and Tours (www. brewster.ca) operates a twice-daily bus service from Calgary International Airport to Lake Louise. Brewster's toll-free number for information is 1-800-661-1152 (Canada and U.S.).

Other companies offer frequent van service between the airport and Banff and Lake Louise, including Banff Airporter (www.airporter.com) 1-888-449-2901 and Rocky Mountain Sky Shuttle (www.rockymountainskyshuttle.com) 1-888-762-8754.

At this writing, there is no public train service to Lake Louise. However, Rocky Mountaineer Vacations (www.rockymountaineer.com) offers a number of packages between late May and early October, including a two-day trip between Vancouver and Banff with overnight in Kamloops. It's toll-free to call them at 1-877-460-3200 (Canada and U.S.).

Major car rental agencies have offices in Lake Louise and Banff. Taxi service is an option to reach trailheads.

There is an entry fee for private vehicles in national parks: the park website gives details; see Information below. Passes are available at park gates, information centres, and the Parks Canada office in Calgary (see Information below).

Lake Louise Village offers such services as a Parks Canada information centre, warden office, Royal Canadian Mounted Police detachment, gas stations, restaurants, a liquor store, a range of accommodation (see p. 14), groceries, a delicatessen and bakery, a bookstore, a post office, outdoor equipment, and other supplies and services (many of them in the Samson Mall).

There is a proposal to develop a low-emissions public transit system to shuttle visitors from the Trans-Canada Highway to Lake Louise and Moraine Lake.

## Information

Visit the Lake Louise Information Centre, operated by Parks Canada, for information on park campgrounds (frontcountry and backcountry), trail conditions, wildlife warnings or closures, weather, the park program of interpretive events, and commercial accommodation. Backcountry campground reservations can be made here, at the Banff Information Centre, and at the Parks Canada office in Calgary.

The Lake Louise Information Centre is located next to Samson Mall, north of the four-way intersection at the entrance to the village, on the west side of Village Road. The phone number is (403) 522-3833. The fax number is (403) 522-1212. Information about the Lake Louise area is also available at the Parks Canada Information Centre in Banff townsite at 224 Banff Avenue; phone (403) 762-1550, fax (403) 762-1551.

The Banff National Park website (www.pc.gc.ca/banff) presents much helpful current information. You can request information by e-mail to: ll.info@pc.gc.ca, or by postal service to: The Superintendent, Banff National Park, P.O. Box 900, Banff, Alberta, Canada T1L 1K2.

Parks Canada produces the *Day Hikes in Banff National Park* and *Backcountry Visitors' Guide, Banff National Park* brochures.

Information on Banff National Park is also available at the Parks Canada Calgary office; phone toll-free 1-800-748-7275 or (403) 292-4401, fax (403) 292-4408. The mailing address is Suite 1550, 635—8th Avenue SW, Calgary, Alberta, Canada T2P 3M3.

Recorded information on Banff National Park trail conditions is available at (403) 760-1305.

The Banff/Lake Louise Tourism Bureau (www.bannflakelouise.com) can help regarding commercial accommodation and attractions in the area. It operates a desk within the Information Centre at 224 Banff Avenue, Banff; phone (403) 762-8421 or write to P.O. Box 1298, Banff, Alberta, Canada T1L 1B3.

The provincial agency Travel Alberta (www.travelalberta.com) offers a travel information service at the toll-free number 1-800-252-3782 (Canada and U.S.), or by mail from Travel Alberta, P.O. Box 2500, Edmonton, Alberta, Canada T5J 2Z4. Travel Alberta operates a seasonal Visitor Information Centre in Field, B.C. (west of Lake Louise) that is primarily intended for personal visits; for information by phone, please use the toll-free number above.

# Accommodation

Parks Canada operates two frontcountry campgrounds in the Lake Louise area. To reach the main Lake Louise campground, head from Lake Louise Village toward the lake itself, but soon turn south (left) off Lake Louise Drive onto Fairview Road just after passing under the railway overpass. Continue straight to the campground kiosk. There are 189 serviced sites in the trailer section (open year round) and from about late June to late September there are 220 semi-serviced sites in the tenting section. The tenting section has kitchen shelters and an outdoor theatre for interpretive programs. There are showers in both sections. A bear-proof fence surrounds the campground. {A plan is in the works for some form of fencing around the entire village.}

The Protection Mountain campground is on the northeast side of the Bow Valley Parkway (Highway 1A), 16.1 km (10.0 mi) southwest from the intersection with the Lake Louise ski area road or 10.4 km (6.4 mi) northwest from Castle Junction. This campground is open from about June until September. There are 89 semi-serviced sites, and kitchen shelters.

There is an overflow camping area beside the Trans-Canada Highway 5.7 km (3.5 mi) south of the Lake Louise interchange and 19.7 km (12.2 mi) north of Castle Junction. This is a noisy location.

There are 10 other frontcountry campgrounds in Banff National Park, at locations including Tunnel Mountain near Banff townsite, Two Jack Lake, Johnston Canyon, Castle Junction, Mosquito Creek, and Waterfowl Lakes. For more information, use the sources above in Information (p. 13).

The Southern Alberta section of Hostelling International-Canada operates a hostel in Lake Louise Village in affiliation with the Alpine Club of Canada. There is a similarly high-standard hostel in Banff townsite, and there are also more rustic hostels at Castle Junction and Mosquito Creek, as well as other locations more distant from Lake Louise. Reservations for the Lake Louise hostel only can be made at (403) 522-2202 or toll-free 1-866-762-4122, or via e-mail at central.res.sa@hihostels.ca. Reserve all other hostels at the toll-free number or the same e-mail address. The Hostelling International-Canada website (www.hihostels.ca) has information on all hostels.

The Alpine Club of Canada (www.alpineclubofcanada.ca) operates a network of alpine huts and shelters, as well as the Canadian Alpine Centre and International Hostel at Lake Louise (the latter in conjunction with Hostelling International-Canada). Most of the ACC's facilities are in remote locations with difficult access, though the Bow Hut near Bow Lake [not far north of Lake Louise] is not hard to reach. For information and reservations, call (403) 678-3200, fax (403) 678-3224, or write to P.O. Box 8040, Canmore, Alberta, Canada T1W 2T8.

There is an extensive network of over 50 backcountry campgrounds in Banff National Park, of which seven are in the area covered by this book. For details on those not in this book, contact Parks Canada as per Information above.

The sole backcountry lodge in the area of Banff National Park covered by this book is Skoki Lodge (www.skokilodge.com or toll-free 1-800-258-7669). See p. 104.

Commercial accommodation in the Lake Louise area ranges from rustic cabins to luxurious hotel rooms. Obtain information at the Lake Louise Information Centre as mentioned above in Information (p. 13).

# Wilderness Pass and Voluntary Safety Registration

Purchase of a Wilderness Pass is mandatory for any overnight backcountry stay in Banff National Park. There is no charge for children 16 and under. The Wilderness Pass specifies the backcountry campground(s) to be used in the Lake Louise area. A Wilderness Pass is required for bivouacing. An Annual Wilderness Pass—valid in all the mountain national parks in Alberta and B.C.—is worth considering if spending seven nights or more in the backcountry over the course of a year. (Trip registration is still required with an Annual Pass.) Purchase a Wilderness Pass at the Parks Canada Information Centres in Lake Louise or Banff (see the Information section p. 13); Information Centres in other national parks can also issue a Wilderness Pass.

Reservations can be made (for a fee) up to 90 days in advance of a backcountry trip by contacting a Parks Canada Information Centre (see Information p. 13). Reservations are recommended for the peak months of July and August if set on a certain itinerary. If the Wilderness Pass is sent by mail or fax, it's suggested to stop at an Information Centre before setting out in order to get updates on trail conditions, wildlife activity, closures, weather, and other pertinent information. Note that Parks Canada policy on managing human use and protecting wildlife has seen changes in backcountry access, and more changes are in the works...check before beginning a trip.

Wilderness Passes can be picked up at Information Centres or at the Parks Canada office in Calgary. Passes not picked up by 10 a.m. on the day of departure will be cancelled and consequent vacancies filled on a first-come, first-served basis. There is no requirement to do anything re. the Wilderness Pass after a trip, but it is highly recommended to leave clear information on the planned route and intended date out with a reliable person, along with who to contact if return is not made by that time.

If planning to engage in an activity involving significant risk, or if there is no one available to notify of your plans, a voluntary safety registration can be made in person when purchasing or picking up the Wilderness Pass. This ensures that, if return is not made by the time indicated, a search will be initiated. A comprehensive and accurate description of the route, including any side trips, must be provided. The onus on the registrant is, of course, to report back immediately upon return: to an Information Centre (if open), otherwise by phone to the Banff Warden Office at (403) 762-1470 (24 hours).

## Climate, Weather, and the Hiking Season

There is a recorded weather forecast for the Banff National Park area at (403) 762-2088 and also at (403) 299-7878 {local call in Calgary area}.

The weather (short-term conditions as compared with the long-term phenomena of climate) in the Lake Louise area—as with any mountain region—is famous for its changeability. British climber Edward Whymper was probably as accurate as most forecasters when, during a 1901 visit to the Canadian Rockies, he renamed the days of the week "Stormday, Rainday, Mistday, Hailday, Thunderday, Snowday, Sleetday." (All of these conditions can even be encountered in one day!)

Always keep in mind the general rule that temperature decreases and precipitation increases with an increase in elevation.                    (cont. next page)

The table below gives data on the climate of the Lake Louise area. Included is information for the months of May through October: daily and extreme maximum and minimum temperatures, average precipitation, and average number of days with measurable precipitation.

Lake Louise Village Climate

|                      | May   | June  | July  | Aug.  | Sept. | Oct.  |
|----------------------|-------|-------|-------|-------|-------|-------|
| Daily max. (°C)      | 12.8  | 16.7  | 20.1  | 19.9  | 14.5  | 7.7   |
| Extreme max. (°C)    | 31.7  | 31.1  | 34.4  | 32.2  | 29.0  | 26.1  |
| Daily min. (°C)      | -1.6  | 2.2   | 3.9   | 3.2   | -0.9  | -5.6  |
| Extreme min. (°C)    | -27.8 | -10.0 | -7.0  | -7.5  | -25.0 | -32.0 |
| Average precip. (mm) | 42.3  | 53.8  | 57.3  | 54.3  | 42.5  | 35.2  |
| Average days precip. | 12    | 16    | 15    | 15    | 11    | 9     |

Source: *Canadian Climate Normals 1971-2000*, Environment Canada.

Note that the figures for average precipitation include both rainfall and snowfall. Snowfall is negligible (usually) in June, July, and August. However, it contributes about one-tenth of the average September precipitation, about one-fifth of May's average precipitation, and over half of October's average precipitation.

Be prepared for sudden changes in weather on any outdoor excursion. The proximity to the high peaks on the continental divide contributes to the Lake Louise area's unpredictable weather. Snowfall has been recorded in all twelve months of the year; deep accumulations of the white stuff make travel difficult and routefinding tricky. Whiteouts (in thick mist) also complicate navigation. Late-lying snowdrifts can remain in high mountain passes, such as Sentinel Pass, well into summer. North-facing slopes take longer to become snow-free after winter.

**Blustery weather in the Valley of the Ten Peaks, with snow on slopes of Mt. Temple.**

The hiking season in the Lake Louise area normally begins in late May, with lower elevation trails opening soonest. Warming temperatures and snowmelt early in the season often lead to wet and muddy conditions, unenjoyable for hiking and often resulting in damage to trails—it's best to confine spring outings to well-constructed, dry trails.

Although clear skies and reasonably mild temperatures often occur in September and October, autumn weather can be especially variable. Heavy, but usually brief, snowstorms are frequent. By mid-October, daytime temperatures have begun to drop, overnight lows fall below freezing, and snow may begin to pile up on the ground. These are all signs that the hiking season has drawn to a close for another year.

## Equipment

There are certain items that should be brought on any outing, including in the Lake Louise area.

It is imperative to have clothing to keep warm and dry: at least a sweater and a rain jacket. It's a good idea to carry rain pants and perhaps long pants if wearing shorts (or wear pants with legs that zip off). Some form of headgear, such as a wool cap, contributes significantly to preventing heat loss. It's surprising how cold fingers can get at higher elevations or if it turns windy; mitts keep hands warmer than gloves.

Use layers (e.g., undershirt, shirt, sweater, jacket) to maintain a comfortable temperature by adding or removing as called for. The secret is to avoid sweating, which can lead to chilling in damp clothing. Garments of breathable material, such as polypropylene or a good Gore-tex membrane, stay drier than cotton or completely waterproof gear that can cause a soaking from the inside. Traditional wool, and new synthetics such as pile and fleece, provide some warmth even when wet.

Be aware that it doesn't take a raging blizzard for hypothermia to happen. That potentially life-threatening drop in body core temperature can occur even when air temperatures are above freezing. For example, a wind speed of 30 km/hr at +4° C creates the equivalent of -8° C. Humidity, dehydration, poor nutrition, and low general fitness can also contribute to the onset of hypothermia.

Footwear should be comfortable and appropriate to the outing. Strolling an easy trail such as the *Lake Louise Lakeshore* in runners is fine, while backpacking —for example up the rough and often muddy *Lower Pipestone Valley* trail—calls for durable boots with good ankle support. This is not to say that heavy "clodhoppers" are necessary for overnight trips...their weight means more work, and their lug sole patterns cause a surprising amount of soil erosion.

Other items to bring on a day hike include effective sunglasses, some kind of sunhat, sunscreen or sunblock (UV radiation and the risk of sunburn increase with elevation), insect repellent, first aid kit, toilet paper, an unbreakable container and/or a hydration system with water or some other drink (preferably nonalcoholic to avoid heat loss), extra food, and a knife such as one of the multi-purpose Swiss Army models.

A map is vital (see the next section); a compass can be very handy. A small flashlight or a headlamp (which has the advantage of leaving hands free) will be well worth the weight if out unexpectedly after dark. Waterproof matches or a lighter, a candle, and a survival blanket can assist in comfortably surviving an emergency.

Backpacking requires all the above, plus lots more. Rather than list all the paraphernalia, the recommendation is to get pointers from sources such as experienced backpackers—perhaps in a club or on a course—or books like **Walking Softly in the Wilderness** by John Hart (Sierra Club Books). This classic also describes excellent techniques for minimum-impact hiking and backcountry camping.

Optional items that can enhance the enjoyment of an outing include camera, binoculars, hand lens, notebook, and sketchpad. There are many field guides to areas of interest such as mammals, wildflowers, birds, trees, and geology. A couple of Luminous Compositions publications fit the bill nicely (they are compact): **Central Rockies Mammals** by John Marriott and **Central Rockies Wildflowers** by Mike Potter. Another good choice is the comprehensive, entertaining **Handbook of the Canadian Rockies** by Ben Gadd (Corax Press, Jasper, Alberta): this covers all the subjects mentioned and much more.

To conclude this section on equipment, it is wise to take to heart these comments by former Park Warden Tim Auger, highly-respected Public Safety Officer for Banff National Park: "The moral of the story is to be prepared to spend at least one night out before help arrives. This is only prudent, since emergency services personnel cannot always respond immediately due to factors such as poor weather or darkness. If properly equipped, a situation such as a simple sprained ankle at Wenkchemna Pass may result in a somewhat uncomfortable night out, but it won't develop into a life-threatening epic."

## Topographic and Geological Maps, and Aerial Photographs

Even though many of the trails described in this book are signed, and—in conjunction with the information provided here—there should be little difficulty keeping on track, it is nevertheless essential to have a more detailed map. This is certainly the case if venturing off-trail.

Maps are also useful for locating landmarks such as peaks, and other features including lakes, rivers, creeks, waterfalls, swamps or marshes, wooded versus open terrain, glaciers, icefields, and moraines. Cliffs and depressions are also marked, as special versions of contour lines: the thin brown lines (close together and wriggly in mountains) that represent a constant elevation. These important sources of information, derived from aerial photographs, enable determination of approximate elevation and also elevation gain or loss. The contour interval on most 1:50,000 maps is 20 or 25 metres (100 feet on old editions). The blue grid lines on 1:50,000 scale maps form two-centimetre squares that correspond to one square kilometre on the ground.

Precise elevations are given for such survey points as bench marks, spot elevations, control points, and surface elevations of large lakes. Topographic maps give the location of cultural (human) features, including roads, railways, bridges, buildings, and boundaries. [The latter don't always have any physical evidence.] **N.B.** Existing trails are sometimes not marked, or locations indicated are incorrect. In some instances, a trail is shown where none exists. The newer the edition the more accurate, usually.

Being able to use grid references is a valuable skill: these numbers derive from the one-kilometre grid (on 1:50,000 sheets) and correspond to a ground location. The use of grid references is explained on the right margin of National Topographic System (NTS) 1:50,000 maps, or get other instruction. **N.B.** Newer maps use the NAD 83 system, in which the same location has a slightly different grid reference from that using the previous NAD 27 system.

There are two good choices of maps for hiking in the Lake Louise area: the Gem Trek Publishing (www.gemtrek.com) series and the government NTS 1:50,000 series. Gem Trek offers "Lake Louise Day Hikes" at 1:35,000 and "Lake Louise & Yoho" at 1:50,000; as well, their "Banff & Mount Assiniboine" at 1:100,000 covers some of the area described in this book. All of the trails and routes in this book fall on the NTS "Lake Louise 82 N/8" map except for these few: those in the Skoki Valley, Red Deer Lakes, and Lower Pipestone Valley areas require the "Hector Lake 82 N/9" sheet, while the *Upper Baker Creek and Pulsatilla Pass* trail calls for the "Castle Mountain 82 O/5" map.

A 1:200,000 scale map of Banff, Kootenay, and Yoho national parks is available. This map, in which each five-centimetre square represents 100 square kilometres on the ground, does not give sufficient detail to be suitable for hiking but can be of use to give a general overview of the area and to identify faraway peaks.

Maps (as well as books and other items) are sold by the Friends of Banff National Park (www.friendsofbanff.com) at their outlets in the two Parks Canada Information Centres. This not-for-profit cooperating association supports many projects in the park; a catalogue can be requested at phone (403) 762-8918, fax (403) 762-2933, or by mail from P.O. Box 2590, Banff, Alberta, Canada T1L 1C3.

Maps are also sold at other locations including The Viewpoint, Book & Art Den, and Mountain Magic Equipment in Banff, Woodruff & Blum Booksellers in Lake Louise, and the Alpine Club of Canada national office in Canmore. In Calgary, Map Town, Mapworld, and Mountain Equipment Co-op are among the choices.

A series of geological maps at 1:50,000 scale published by the Geological Survey of Canada gives fascinating information on the complex, intriguing geological formations of some areas of Banff National Park. (Complimentary "structure sections" showing cross-sections of the mountains accompany the maps.) Contact the GSC Bookstore, 3303 - 33rd St. NW, Calgary, Alberta, Canada T2L 2A7; phone (403) 292-7030.

Aerial photographs are available from the National Air Photo Library (www.airphotos.nrcan.gc.ca). The mailing address is Room 180, 615 Booth Street, Ottawa, Ontario, Canada K1A 0E9; or phone toll-free 1-800-230-6275.

## Safety

The activities described in this guidebook are not inherently dangerous but do hold an element of risk. To be safe, always practise common sense and be aware of potential pitfalls and act accordingly. As stated in the *Backcountry Visitors' Guide* produced by Banff National Park: "Your safety is your personal responsibility. Caution and self-reliance are essential. You or your trip leader should have a knowledge of natural hazards, experience in avoiding them, and a plan to deal with them successfully when required."

The best approach is to be as well informed as possible before heading out, and to choose trips based on personal capabilities and experience. One suggestion is to try a shakedown trip first if new to (or rusty at) an activity. Pushing to the limit can reduce enjoyment of any activity and lead to problems.

In addition to points mentioned above (such as using proper equipment, being prepared for weather changes, having a good map, and possibly taking out a voluntary safety registration), following is information on several topics of particular relevance to safety.

**Bear warning sign.**

**Bears**—Both black bears and grizzly bears occur in the Lake Louise area of Banff National Park. Bears are naturally wary of humans and generally choose to avoid them. However, bears may threaten and even attack people when accustomed to humans, when surprised, or when defending themselves, their young, or food.

Park information centres and warden offices have information on bear sightings and on areas that have been posted with bear warnings or area closures due to bear activity.

It's difficult, because of the many possible factors involved, to give succinct information on how to avoid bears and on how to act in the rare situation of an encounter with a bear. Bears are very intelligent and complex animals; each bear and any encounter is unique. There is no single strategy that will work in all situations. Below follows some general background. For more detailed information, read the excellent book **Bear Attacks: Their Causes and Avoidance** by Dr. Stephen Herrero. It gives much practical information on bear biology, and on precautions and actions to take in a multitude of situations. Dr. Herrero, a former professor at the University of Calgary, is an internationally recognized authority on bears who has done extensive field work in Banff National Park.

The Parks Canada brochure *Keep the Wild in Wildlife* has information on how to reduce the risk of bear encounters. If not received when entering the park, this brochure is available at park frontcountry campgrounds and at information centres.

Interpretive programs can give good information on bears.

An important step is to know how to distinguish between a black bear and a grizzly bear. The most noticeable identifying characteristics of a grizzly bear are the prominent hump at the shoulders and the long, gradually curved claws, neither of which are present in black bears. Colour is not a reliable way to tell the two species apart: black bears can be black or brown, while grizzly bears can be black, blond, or a "silver-tipped" brown.

In general, the best thing to do when travelling in bear country is to take preventive measures. Learn to recognize sign (tracks, scat, diggings, torn-up logs, overturned rocks) and likely habitat (e.g., berry patches, avalanche paths), and change plans if warranted. Stumbling upon a dead animal should lead to the quick decision to clear out; a concentration of ravens can be a sign of a kill. {Report this to Parks Canada.}

It is safer to travel in a group of at least three. Keep children within reach. Travel during daylight hours, and stick to established trails where possible.

Make lots of noise {clap, call out, sing, talk loudly, whatever} while hiking, especially in places where it would be hard to be seen, heard, or smelled by a bear, e.g., among dense vegetation, near a rushing stream, or if there is a headwind. The idea here is to alert any bear, for once aware it will most often leave the area—possibly without even having signalled its presence. Note that bear bells, though popular, are not much use in situations such as high wind or rushing water that drown out their sound.

When camping (both frontcountry and backcountry), keep a fastidiously clean campsite. Cook downwind well away—at least 100 metres—from sleeping quarters. Wash and store all dishes and utensils immediately after use. Strain food particles from dishwater and store with garbage. Dump dishwater in designated sumps, or at least 100 metres from sleeping areas. Do not burn or bury garbage: pack it out in airtight containers and treat it the same way as food in terms of storage.

Keep sleeping bags and tents completely free of food, beverages, and associated odours. Don't sleep in clothes worn while cooking.

Overnight or while away from a tent, store away food and anything else with a strong odour (e.g., food scraps, garbage, cooking pots, stove, dirty dishcloths, and toiletries such as toothpaste, soap, and deodorant if used). Storage should be up the bear-proof systems provided at designated backcountry campgrounds. There is no random camping—which requires a rope to rig a personal storage system—in the area covered in this book. Proper storage will also prevent raids by small animals.

If a bear is seen in the distance, observe it. Wait to see whether it moves away. If so, advance cautiously. Back away and move off slowly if the bear stays on the trail ahead or if it comes closer. Leave the area, or perhaps take a detour to proceed. Always leave a bear an escape route.

**Never** run away from a bear. Bears can run as fast as a racehorse, both uphill and downhill.

Stay calm in a bear situation. Keep together if in a group and immediately pick up any small children. Back away slowly, perhaps speaking calmly and firmly to establish yourself as a human and not a prey animal. A scream or sudden movement may trigger an attack. Avoid direct eye contact, which a bear could perceive as threatening. A pack can provide protection in case of an attack, although shedding a pack can assist in climbing if there is a suitable tree to escape a grizzly bear (see below) and the dropped pack could serve as a distraction.

Climbing a tree may be a possible escape, though black bears climb readily and subadult grizzlies can do so (contrary to widespread belief). Adult grizzly bears can sometimes get up a short distance, and can reach up as high as three metres (10 ft) without taking their hind feet off the ground. The minimum recommended safe height is 10 metres (33 ft).

Black bears are agile tree climbers, using the short, curved claws that may have evolved to allow them to escape grizzly bears, their worst natural enemies. However, although incidents have been recorded in which a black bear pursued an attack upon a person up a tree, this is not the norm.

If there is no suitable tree, a cliff or a lake may offer an avenue of escape (though bears do swim).

Most bears don't attack; they usually try to avoid humans or to ensure that they don't represent a threat. A bear may rear up on its hind legs and wave its nose about in an attempt at identification. A bear may make a bluff charge in which it veers away at close quarters.

If contact is imminent, use bear spray if at hand. Do realize that the effectiveness of bear spray is not guaranteed. For a start, it has to be readily available, preferably in an easily reached holster. Recent research indicates that bear spray can be effective against some bears when used properly. However, wind, spray distance, rain, and product shelf life can all affect how well it works. Carefully read directions beforehand, and don't allow possession of bear spray to let cockiness prevail.

If contact occurs, play dead. Lie face down with legs spread and elbows out to prevent being rolled over. Protect the neck and back of the head with the hands. Remain still until the bear leaves the area. Fighting usually increases the intensity of an attack, although in some cases it has caused the bear to leave. An attack seldom lasts more than a few minutes; if it persists for more than several minutes, consider fighting.

However, if a bear stalks and attacks, or attacks at night, do **not** play dead. In this case, try to escape, possibly up a tree. Use spray, shout, wave a branch, throw rocks...do whatever it takes to let the bear know it isn't looking at easy prey. This kind of attack is rare but can be very serious since it often means that the bear is looking for food and might even consider a human as prey.

Bears are integral and important members of the ecological communities of national parks and wilderness areas. Although they should be accorded a healthy respect as powerful and unpredictable wild creatures, they should not be feared. Knowledge will give an understanding and appreciation of these animals, allowing enjoyment of appropriate activities.

With correct practises, it's unlikely a bear will even be seen on a trail or in the backcountry. Ironically, the best chance of sighting a bear may be along park roads. (There, too, proper steps must be followed for mutual safety.)

**Other animals**—Cougars live in Banff National Park. Although not often seen because of their usually solitary, elusive nature and nocturnal preferences, there is the possibility of an encounter with one. Cougars may be more active near areas such as towns and campgrounds that have habituated prey. The best measures, as with bears, are preventive, so make noise and travel in a group if possible. Keep children close at hand, and immediately pick up a small child if a cougar is sighted. With a cougar, do **not** play dead and do not run. Face the animal and retreat slowly, increasing apparent size by raising arms or an object overhead. Be aggressive to deter an attack: shout, wave a stick, throw stones.

To date other large carnivores such as wolves and wolverines have not represented a safety hazard to hikers or backpackers in Banff National Park.

Coyotes have inflicted minor injuries to young people and to people sleeping out in the open; these incidents have usually occurred in areas where coyotes have become habituated to humans (such as near townsites or campgrounds).

Elk are dangerous, especially during calving season (mid-May to the end of June) when cow elk are protective of their young, and during mating season (mid-September to the end of October) when bull elk are aggressive. Parks Canada recommends staying at least 30 metres (100 ft) away from elk at all times—this distance is equal to three bus lengths.

Moose are even bigger than elk, and if sighted should also be given a wide berth.

Ground squirrels can inflict a sharp bite, so abide by park regulations prohibiting feeding or enticing them.

**Ticks**—The Rocky Mountain wood tick is a small (about 5 mm or 1/4 inch long), mostly reddish-brown, flat-bodied, eight-legged arachnid: of the same class as spiders but in a different order. Ticks, which need mammal blood as part of their life cycle, are often abundant on animals such as elk, moose, and bighorn sheep, to which they usually do little harm.

However, ticks will also attempt to use humans as hosts, and can induce paralysis or transmit potentially fatal Rocky Mountain spotted fever.

Ticks are most active in Banff National Park from April to June. They occur most often on dry, grassy slopes—especially those frequented by ground squirrels—up to about 2100 metres (almost 7000 ft) elevation. As preventive measures against ticks, wear long pants tucked into socks and don't sit or stretch out in areas likely to harbour ticks. An insect repellent containing DEET can be applied to clothing that will come into contact with grasses or low shrubs. Ticks do not drop from trees.

After any outing, check thoroughly—and help any companions check—for ticks that may have hitched a ride. Look especially carefully around the head and neck, in other hairy areas, and where clothing is constricted. Ticks usually spend at least three hours looking for a place to draw off blood, generally climbing up in their search, so there is a good chance of brushing them off before they inflict any damage. (Ticks do not sting.) If at home or in a place where a tick might return for another try, it should be flushed down the toilet or crushed with footwear or a solid object (**not** fingers); this isn't necessary on a hike.

If a tick has become attached and begun feeding (which it does by painlessly inserting its mouthparts through the skin), the best procedure is to remove the whole body by pulling steadily but gently. Grasp it near the head to try to get the mouthparts out. Don't try such folk remedies as burning the tick's rear or dousing it with alcohol: this will only kill it while still embedded. If the mouthparts stay in, remove them by teasing out with a heated needle or knife. Then wash the wound thoroughly with soap and sterilize it with antiseptic if possible.

If a tick has fed, the person should see a doctor. If it has remained unnoticed for several days, signs of tick paralysis may develop: numbness in the extremities, loss of coordination, and drowsiness. These conditions clear up within a few hours once the tick is removed.

In the rare case of infection with potentially fatal Rocky Mountain spotted fever, a high temperature, severe headache, chills, muscle pain, and a cough will ensue. Later a rash usually covers the arms and legs, and sometimes other parts of the body. Get immediate treatment if any of these symptoms appear.

To alleviate concerns (without of course dismissing the future possibility), it may be a relief to learn that there have been no cases of tick paralysis or Rocky Mountain spotted fever reported from Banff National Park in over 15 years.

At time of writing, there have been no confirmed cases of Lyme disease traceable to Alberta, but it may appear soon. It is usually transmitted by tiny (pinhead-sized) deer ticks, which are now present but so far do not carry the disease.

**Hantavirus**—Droppings and urine from mice can contain potentially deadly hantavirus. Infection initially causes flu-like symptoms, with shortness of breath and increased heart rate later developing. Over 60 percent of untreated cases result in death from lungs filled with fluid.

Store food as securely as possible, and wear rubber gloves and a respirator if cleaning up after mice in places such as a trail shelter or an alpine hut.

**Water**—Drinking water is a safety concern in the backcountry due to the possibility of giardiasis, the ailment commonly known as "beaver fever." Despite their pristine appearance, the streams, rivers, and lakes of Banff National Park can harbour the protozoan parasite *Giardia lamblia*.

The symptoms of *Giardia* infection do not appear until 10 to 15 days after contamination. They include diarrhoea, stomach cramps, poor appetite, and general lethargy. If these signs appear and giardiasis is suspected, see a doctor.

As always, the best approach is to take preventive measures. To avoid this illness, use an appropriate portable filter or boil for at least five minutes all water for drinking, cooking, and personal hygiene. Practise good sanitation, including using out-houses where available. If there is no loo, defecate at least 100 metres away from any water source, digging a small hole 15-20 cm deep and covering it afterward. The title may sound flippant, but an entire book has been written on the subject of proper out-door human waste disposal practises: **How to Shit in the Woods** (Kathleen Meyer, Ten Speed Press).

Be careful to avoid dehydration.

**Fords**—In a different context from drinking, water can present another hazard: that of crossing streams and rivers on foot. Fords can be a tricky business: drowning due to a slip while trying to negotiate a high, swift-flowing, numbingly cold mountain torrent is a distinct possibility. Many of the backcountry trails in the Lake Louise area that entail fords are best left for late summer when the season's heaviest snowmelt is over. Also be aware that sudden rainfall, or high temperatures causing increased glacial melt, can also make fords difficult.

Prepare for any such crossing by finding a pole (or using an ice axe or solid walking pole) to serve as a third point of contact and to provide support. The recommendation is to plant the brace upstream and face into the current while crossing. If in a group, link arms and/or wrap them around a pole held horizontally.

It's a good idea to carry lightweight runners or sports sandals: they are nice to change into at the end of a day of backpacking, plus can serve for crossings. They give better purchase than bare feet, particularly on slippery rocks or in cold water. If those conditions prevail and there is no alternative, crossing in boots is wise. Put on dry spare socks afterward, and hopefully dry out the footwear overnight if on a backpacking trip (e.g., at the campfire if permitted).

Before heading across a ford, make sure everything is secure—the exception being a backpack waistbelt, which should be left undone so that it can be dumped quickly if trouble arises. If the current becomes too strong or too high in the course of an attempted crossing, retreat and look for a wider (thus usually shallower) place to ford. Or wait for the water level to drop, as it will after a sudden rainstorm has passed or by early morning on a glacially fed watercourse if there have been warm midday temperatures.

If a ford is not feasible, discretion is the better part of valour: back off and perhaps choose another route.

**Lightning**—This powerful natural phenomenon poses significant danger to outdoor enthusiasts. Its frequency is attested to by the fact that around the globe there are up to 100 lightning strikes per second.

Warning signs that lightning may be about to strike in the immediate vicinity include a sensation of itchy skin, hair moving and standing out, and crackling sounds from metal objects such as an ice axe or fishing rod.

The chances of being hit by the main path of a lightning bolt, which is often deadly, are remote. Many people struck by secondary paths—not as powerful as the main path but still packing a wallop—do survive.

The main danger from being hit by lightning is cardiac arrest. The strike can short-circuit the heart's electrical system, and the heart may not spontaneously restart. Anyone who is conscious immediately after being hit by lightning will almost certainly recover, but a lightning strike victim who is unconscious is probably in cardiac arrest and requires immediate CPR (cardiopulmonary resuscitation) and medical attention.

The following suggestions will not guarantee avoiding lightning (like many natural forces, it is unpredictable), but they will improve the odds against being hit:

— Never take shelter under an isolated tree: this mistake claims the single largest group of lightning fatalities. If lightning strikes the tree, a secondary discharge or ground current could hit anyone beneath. In addition, lightning can cause instant vaporization of the sap, exploding the tree.

— During a thunderstorm, don't become the tallest object around by standing in an open area. If forced to stay in the open, look for a depression in which to crouch down. Keep feet together to minimize the danger from ground current.

— If on a ridge, head down.

— Move away from open water since people are often the highest object in such an area.

— Set aside any metal objects, such as an ice axe or fishing rod. These do not attract lightning but can result in burns.

**Off-trail travel**—Travel beyond established trails, such as on any of the scrambles described in this book, requires awareness of such natural hazards as cliffs and canyons, and unstable scree, talus, and moraines. Other dangers include rockfall, cornices (windblown deposits of snow hanging out from a ridge over nothing but air—don't venture near their edges), and avalanches (yes, even in spring and summer; spontaneous cornice collapse due to weakening in warm temperatures is one cause).

An ice axe is necessary to travel on steep snow, and of course it should be more than just decoration...knowledge of how to self-arrest is what it's for, to prevent an out-of-control slide toward a cliff or jagged rocks. Take a course or get pointers from someone who knows. Avoid icy gullies or slopes that may have ice under a thin layer of snow.

Note that to attempt an off-trail scramble requires good routefinding skills, including map-and-compass navigation where necessary. Equipment has to be in good condition. The terrain negotiated on off-trail scrambles can include boulderfields, trackless forest, and featureless alpine meadows. On all scrambles, it is essential to keep impact to a minimum.

The scope of this guidebook does not include glacier travel, which calls for specialized equipment and knowledge of specific hazards including crevasses, moulins (millwells), and glacier caves.

**Cornices on summit ridge of Mt. Temple (Moraine Lake below).**

## Interpretive Events

Parks Canada staff offer a slate of events that can give insights into the natural and human heritage of the Lake Louise area. These include guided walks and hikes, evening programs, films, roving exhibits, and special events. Some of these are free (sometimes with limited space), others have a charge. A schedule of regular events is given in *The Mountain Guide* newsletter. Information centres and frontcountry campgrounds also have this information.

Interpretive events and programs are also presented by a number of private businesses, including Great Divide Nature Interpretation, P.O. Box 343, Lake Louise, Alberta, Canada T0L 1E0; toll-free 1-866-522-2735 (website www.greatdivide.ca).

## Other Activities

In addition to the activities described in this book, there are many other self-propelled pursuits to enjoy in the Lake Louise area.. These include mountain biking (subject to restrictions), bicycle touring, rockclimbing, mountaineering, canoeing, kayaking, and winter activities such as cross-country skiing and snowshoeing.

Abundant information on these topics is available at park information centres and in other publications.

## Some Relevant National Park Regulations

In addition to the requirements mentioned above, such as the mandatory Wilderness Pass for overnight trips, there are other rules to follow while in Banff National Park: these are for everyone's benefit, including the wildlife.

— Within the backcountry, zoning (e.g., Outdoor Recreation, Natural Environment, Wilderness, and Special Preservation) governs overnight camping. Designated backcountry campgrounds must be used in the zones where they are provided, which includes all of the areas described in this book.

— Fires are only permitted at certain backcountry campgrounds, where the metal fireboxes provided must be used. If the choice is to have a fire, keep it small and use only deadfall. Tend a fire at all times and douse it completely before leaving. Lightweight backpacking stoves are recommended for cooking as they are clean and efficient; they are obligatory if there is a fire ban or if at a backcountry campground where fires are prohibited.

— Dogs must be restrained on a leash at all times in a national park. Pets may provoke a confrontation with wildlife such as bears or cougars; they can also attract wood ticks. It might be better to leave pets at home.

— Feeding, enticing, touching, or harassing wildlife are prohibited; conviction can result in a substantial fine. Feeding an animal interferes with its natural foraging and can cause habituation, in which the animal loses its natural wariness around humans. This can affect its survival and lead to injury to people. Most people are well aware of the illegality of feeding wildlife, particularly bears; it applies equally to smaller creatures such as ground squirrels and gray jays.

— Leave all wildflowers, plants, trees, rocks, fossils, horns, antlers, nests, eggs, and any other natural or historical objects undisturbed—for others to enjoy and since that is where they belong.

— The "pack-in, pack-out" policy is in force in national parks: do not leave behind any garbage on an outing. Do not bury food scraps, which can easily be discovered and dug up by wildlife. If you dispose of garbage in a fire (where permitted), burn only combustible matter and ensure that it is completely consumed. Anything not quickly biodegradable should be packed out. A free litter bag is issued with the Wilderness Pass required for overnight trips. Good planning will keep the amount of garbage generated on a trip to a minimum. Good stewardship suggests taking out any garbage left by others, to leave an area better than found.

— A valid national parks fishing licence is required to go angling within a national park. Licences can be purchased at locations such as Parks Canada information centres and the Parks Canada office in Calgary (see p. 13).

— The use of firearms in national parks is illegal. Any firearms in transport must be kept sealed and unloaded, with ammunition stored separately. Firearms cannot be taken onto any trail or into the backcountry. A Wildlife Watch program is in effect in Banff National Park. Call 911 in Banff National Park to immediately report suspicious activity or a poaching incident (or any violation of park regulations). [Other options are to call toll-free 1-888-WARDENS (927-3367), or in a non-emergency situation (403) 762-1470.] If witness to an infraction, observe from a distance and get as many details as possible but don't endanger personal safety.

## Some Final Suggestions

Here are some pointers that may be helpful:

— It's generally recommended not to travel alone in the outdoors, for reasons of safety. Sharing observations and experiences can enhance an outing.

— When on established trails, keep to the path. Avoid shortcutting, which is hard on the environment and ultimately harder on the body. Shortcuts, especially on switchbacks, cause erosion and lead to maintenance problems. So does the unnecessary creation of new trails: wear appropriate footwear and think about impact. Even if there are muddy sections, stay on the beaten path. Prevent unsightly and destructive trail braiding.

— If in a group travelling off-trail, disperse rather than concentrate, i.e., spread out rather than going single file. Choose a route to avoid trampling vegetation as much as possible by passing over rock or bare ground.

— When backpacking, use a tent with a waterproof floor and a rainfly. Refrain from trenching, and definitely do not follow the archaic practice of making a bough bed (cutting live branches to sleep on)...that idea belongs to the Dark Ages. Instead take an inflatable sleeping pad (e.g., Therm-a-Rest) or a closed cell foam pad.

— Do any washing—of dishes, of clothes, personal hygiene—well away from water sources (at least 100 metres). Pour any dirty or soapy water into a waste sump or a shallow hole that is covered over; don't introduce it directly into water sources. Ditto for toothpaste.

— Do not tempt a porcupine attracted to salt by leaving around gear such as boots and backpacks with leather attachment points. Also, close and latch outhouse doors upon leaving; otherwise, a porcupine could damage the interior.

— Don't take cans or bottles on backpacking trips, because of weight, possibility of breakage, and garbage concerns. If necessary, repackage food into required quantities. Pouch-packed and freeze-dried foods are usually lightweight, tasty, and reasonably priced. Pick a menu that requires the least possible amount of cooking, thus conserving fuel as well as saving time. Choose food that does not give off strong, animal-attracting odours (fish and meat have drawbacks in this regard). Try to gauge consumption so that all of a meal will be eaten; this reduces leftovers or garbage. If possible, cook meals for which clean-up is easy.

— Be environmentally responsible with respect to outdoor activities (seems obvious, doesn't it?). Practise the credo of "reduce, re-use, recycle." Take advantage of recycling facilities (such as in Lake Louise, Banff, and Canmore) for such materials as paper, newsprint, cardboard, tin, glass, and redeemable beverage containers. If in a private vehicle, observe the speed limit. Speeding wastes gasoline and endangers wildlife and people (including speeders); besides, a big reason for getting outdoors is usually to relax! Another conservation measure is to take into account the amount of driving for a given hike: does it make sense to drive for hours for a 20 minute walk? Several short outings could be combined over a couple of days or so.

Overall, the slogan "Be prepared" holds true. Observing this simple advice often makes the difference between a rewarding outing and a disappointing one.

As pioneer explorer and climber Walter Wilcox wrote in *Camping in the Canadian Rockies* (1896): "Mountain adventures (...) comprise all the scale of sensations, from those marked by the pains of extreme exhaustion, physical weakness, hunger, and cold, to those of the greatest exhilaration and pleasure. Fortunately, the sensations of pleasure are by far the more abundant."

**Early summer scene at Lower Consolation Lake with ice still floating about; Panorama Ridge above and Mt. Bell in the distance on the right.**

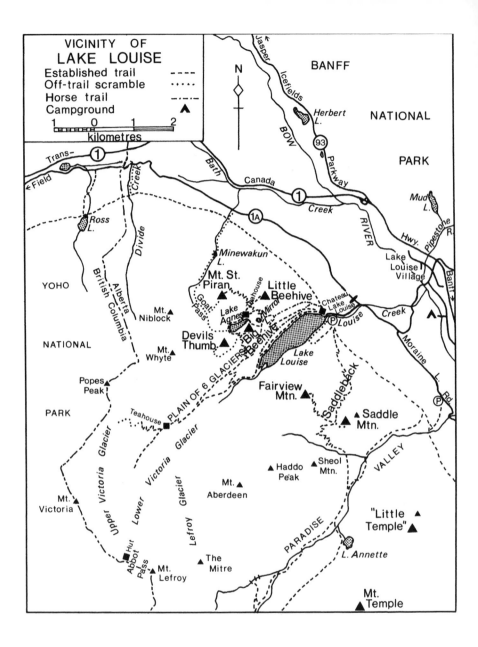

VICINITY OF
**LAKE LOUISE**
Established trail
Off-trail scramble
Horse trail
Campground ▲

1  0  1  2
kilometres

N

BANFF

NATIONAL

PARK

Jasper
Icefields
Herbert L.
BOW
93
Parkway

Trans-
Field
Canada
1
Creek
1A

Mud L.

Ross L.
Divide

Bath
Creek

Lake
Louise
Village

Hwy. Pipestone R.

Banff

YOHO

Alberta
British Columbia

Mt.
Niblock

Minewakun L.

Mt. St.
Piran

Goat Pass

Lake
Agnes

Teahouse

Mirror

Little
Beehive

Chateau
Lake Louise
P
Louise

Creek

Moraine

L.
Rd.

P

NATIONAL

Mt.
Whyte

Devils
Thumb

Big
Beehive

Lake
Louise

Popes
Peak

PLAIN OF 6 GLACIERS

Teahouse

PARK

Upper Victoria Glacier

Lower Victoria Glacier

Fairview
Mtn.

Saddleback

Saddle
Mtn.

Lefroy Glacier

Haddo
Peak

Sheol
Mtn.

VALLEY

Mt.
Aberdeen

Mt.
Victoria

Abbot Hut
Pass

Mt.
Lefroy

The
Mitre

PARADISE

L. Annette

"Little
Temple"

Mt.
Temple

30

# Vicinity of Lake Louise

**On the ledge section of *The Plain of Six Glaciers* trail, looking to (l to r) Mt. Lefroy and Mt. Victoria.**

# Lake Louise Lakeshore

See cover photo.

**Distance:** 1.9 km (1.2 mi) — Chateau Lake Louise to west end of Lake Louise
**Walk:** 30 minutes one way
**Elevation gain:** 10 m (35 ft)
**Maximum elevation:** 1740 m (5705 ft)
**Trailhead:** The northeast corner of Lake Louise; pass in front of the Chateau Lake Louise after crossing from the large public parking areas using either of two footbridges over Louise Creek. Lake Louise is 5.0 km (3.1 mi) from Lake Louise Village in the valley—from the Lake Louise exit on the Trans-Canada Highway, go west and keep straight at two four-way stops to head uphill on Lake Louise Drive. The parking areas are to the left past Deer Lodge and just before the Chateau Lake Louise (don't take the right turn to the Chateau).

0.0 — Sign at junction (elevation 1730 m). Stay to the left along the north shore of Lake Louise on a wide, level trail.

1.6 —-Small boat dock. Begin short climb.

1.7 — Junction with horse route that parallels this trail through forest. Continue straight.

1.9 — Viewpoint with rest bench (1740 m) at west end of Lake Louise. *The Plain of Six Glaciers* trail continues from here (see p. 34).

This walk along the north shore of Lake Louise gives a relaxing introduction to this, perhaps the most famous body of water in the Canadian Rockies.

**Hikers near the west end of the *Lake Louise Lakeshore* trail, looking ahead to the 'Back of the Lake' cliffs and Mt. Lefroy.**

**Least chipmunk.**

**Golden-mantled ground squirrel.**

Visitors continue to be as impressed as Tom Wilson, who in 1882 became the first non-Native to see Lake Louise. He wrote: "I never, in all my explorations of these five chains of mountains throughout Western Canada, saw such a matchless scene. I felt puny in body but glorified in spirit and soul."

As well as the beauty of Lake Louise, there are two common species of wildlife that can usually be observed at the beginning of this trail. One is a small mammal: the golden-mantled ground squirrel, which has stripes on its back (but not on its head like the smaller-still chipmunk). The other is a bird: the Clark's nutcracker, looking somewhat like a gray jay but with a longer bill plus black-and-white highlights. This member of the crow family has a typically raucous call, and is resourceful but nevertheless endearing.

At a rest bench 400 metres from the start is a fine view of the Chateau Lake Louise. The mountains in the distance across the Bow Valley present a natural scene here, which is not the case farther along. This viewpoint also gives a good indication of the fact that Lake Louise lies in a hanging valley. Common in the Canadian Rockies, such valleys were created by the scouring action of tributary glaciers that did not carve as deeply as major glaciers. In this case, the valley of Lake Louise "hangs" above the Bow Valley, with Lake Louise Village some 200 metres lower in elevation. The Chateau Lake Louise sits on a lateral (side) moraine left by the Bow Valley glacier; this ancient ridge served to dam Lake Louise.

The trail along the lakeshore follows a winding course beside small indentations that are not apparent from a distance. South across Lake Louise is a large cone of talus below the cliff band of Fairview Mountain (see photo p. 42). This material falls after being loosened by frost wedging, caused by water seeping into cracks and then levering out pieces of rock as it expands in freezing. This constitutes a safety hazard, which is why the faint trail barely discernible on the south side of the lake is closed and no longer maintained.

There is a short incline after the small boat dock at km 1.6, after which the trail passes beneath purplish quartzite cliffs, known to rock climbers as the 'Back of the Lake.' A variety of technically demanding climbing routes have been put up on these overhanging walls of rock.

And the lake's name? It is generally accepted to be in honour of Princess Louise Caroline Alberta, fourth daughter of Queen Victoria and wife of the Marquis of Lorne, Governor General of Canada from 1878 to 1883. The province of Alberta is also named after the princess.

# The Plain of Six Glaciers

See photos p. 5, p. 31, p. 51, and eighth page of colour photos starting opposite p. 64.

**Distance:** 3.6 km (2.2 mi) — End of *Lake Louise Lakeshore* trail to the Plain of Six Glaciers teahouse
**Day hike:** 1.5 hours one way
**Elevation gain:** 360 m (1180 ft)
**Maximum elevation:** 2100 m (6890 ft)
**Trailhead:** End of the *Lake Louise Lakeshore* trail (see two previous pages).

0.0 — End of the *Lake Louise Lakeshore* trail at a rest bench (elevation 1740 m) above the west end of Lake Louise. Descend a short distance to travel beside the braided channels of Louise Creek.

0.4 — Begin gradual climb at two rest benches where Louise Creek is a single stream between rocky banks.

1.4 — Junction (1840 m) with bottom of *Shortcut Switchbacks to The Plain of Six Glaciers trail* from the *Highline* trail (see p. 39). Keep straight.

2.2 — Junction (1950 m) with the *Highline* trail for Lake Agnes (see p. 38). Keep left. The trail stays fairly level before heading along a narrow ledge (there is an alternate route along the base of the cliff). Then begin a steady climb in the trough behind the north lateral moraine of the Lower Victoria Glacier.

3.3 — Series of four short switchbacks.

3.6 — Plain of Six Glaciers teahouse (2100 m) a short distance to the right.

The essentially flat *Lake Louise Lakeshore* trail (see two previous pages) serves as a good warm-up for this outing. At first this trail runs along the delta at the west end of Lake Louise, perpetually forming as particles of silt carried in the rushing meltwater streams settle out when they reach still water.

Where the trail begins to climb, a sign marked "End of Nordic Ski Trail" suggests the origin of the open swaths soon encountered: they are avalanche chutes. Snow released from the cliffs above rushes down the slopes, keeping them clear of vegetation and representing a safety hazard to outdoor enthusiasts, especially cross-country skiers.

**Young hoary marmot photographed on *The Plain of Six Glaciers* trail.**

**The Plain of Six Glaciers teahouse.**

Hoary marmots, large grey members of the rodent family with reddish tails as adults, are often found in the slide-cleared meadows. Marmots are sometimes referred to as "whistlers" because of their high-pitched, far-carrying alarm calls.

After the junction at km 1.4, there are views of the terminal moraine left by the most recent advance of the Lower Victoria Glacier during the Little Ice Age, which peaked circa 1850. The present outlet stream flows through the steep, narrow gorge it has breached in the material deposited at the toe of the receding glacier.

The third in a series of four short switchbacks just 300 m before the teahouse grants an excellent perspective over the toe of the Lower Victoria Glacier (which often sports a glacial cave), and across to the peak named The Mitre—shaped like a bishop's cap—between Mt. Aberdeen and Mt. Lefroy.

The Plain of Six Glaciers teahouse is the original structure, opened in 1924.

Arrival at the teahouse reveals the half dozen glaciers that give the teahouse and this trail their names: hanging glaciers on mts. Aberdeen, Lefroy, and Victoria; the Lefroy and Lower Victoria valley glaciers; and finally the bulge of a hanging glacier to the north on Popes Peak.

Subalpine larch trees grow near the teahouse. Larches are unique in that although they are conifers, they shed all their needles in the autumn. The needles turn a brilliant golden hue before dropping off. Each year's soft-textured subalpine larch foliage grows anew starting in spring.

The Plain of Six Glaciers teahouse is also near the high cliff haunts of mountain goats, with their white coats and thin black horns. These sturdy, stocky climbers, which rely on seemingly insurmountable walls as escape terrain, can often be observed on the slopes due north of the teahouse.

See the next two pages for optional extensions to this hike.

# Abbot Pass Viewpoint

See photo p. 7.

**Distance:** 1.3 km (0.8 mi) — Plain of Six Glaciers teahouse to Abbot Pass view-
point
**Extension of day hike:** 30 minutes one way
**Elevation gain:** 50 m (165 ft)
**Maximum elevation:** 2150 m (7050 ft)
**Trailhead:** Plain of Six Glaciers teahouse (see two previous pages).

0.0 — Plain of Six Glaciers teahouse (elevation 2100 m). At the end of *The Plain of Six Glaciers* trail, where turn right for the teahouse, instead keep left.
0.1 — Cross small stream on a footbridge.
0.2 — Keep straight (2105 m); faint path of *Upper Victoria Glacier Access* trail to right (see page opposite).
1.1 — The edge of a lateral moraine. **N.B.** The final 200 m is along the unstable crest of the moraine, with a steep drop to the left.
1.3 — Viewpoint (2150 m) up to Abbot Pass.

This extension to *The Plain of Six Glaciers* trail leads beyond the teahouse to a view of historic but usually hidden Abbot Pass. This lofty saddle lies between mts. Lefroy and Victoria; the continental divide, which runs along their crests, dips down to the pass. Water falling on the west side of the peaks and the pass flows to the Pacific Ocean, while rivers originating on the east side ultimately reach the Atlantic.

The name of the pass commemorates Philip Stanley Abbot, a young climber from Boston who died in a fall on adjacent Mt. Lefroy in 1896: the first mountaineering fatality in North America.

Visible against the skyline is the Alpine Club of Canada's Abbot Pass Hut, a solid structure of stone built by Swiss guides in 1922. At an elevation of over 2900 m, this was the highest permanent shelter in Canada until the recent construction of another hut in the Moraine Lake area. (In truth, the outhouse—which has a rope leading to it as a handrail, necessary in high winds or poor visibility—deserved the honour!)

Changes in ice conditions have made access to Abbot Pass Hut from the Lake Louise side even more hazardous than it used to be. The somewhat macabre but accurate name of The Deathtrap for the couloir beneath the pass gives a sobering idea of the other dangers from avalanches and rockfall. It's still no cakewalk, but the usual way up to Abbot Pass is from Lake O'Hara to the west in Yoho National Park, B.C.

**Telephoto view of Abbot Pass Hut (and outhouse to right). Note avalanches across track on left.**

# Upper Victoria Glacier Access

See photo p. 7.

**Distance:** 1.8 km (1.1 mi) — *Abbot Pass Viewpoint* trail to Upper Victoria Glacier access
**Extension of day hike and off-trail scramble:** 1 hour one way
**Elevation gain:** 640 m (2100 ft)
**Maximum elevation:** 2745 m (9005 ft)
**Trailhead:** Km 0.2 of *Abbot Pass Viewpoint* trail (see page opposite).

0.0 — Junction on *Abbot Pass Viewpoint* trail (elevation 2105 m) at the west edge of a large avalanche path. Turn right on a faint path and begin a series of steep switchbacks.

1.0 — End of established trail on a small plateau (2440 m).

1.8 — Reach edge of upper lobe of Upper Victoria Glacier (2745 m) after scrambling higher, above a well-defined lateral moraine.

This outing, starting on a trail established by Swiss guides in the 1920s as the initial section of a climber's access route to the Upper Victoria Glacier, provides a dramatic perspective on the surroundings.

The narrow path, somewhat overgrown in places, climbs steadily — at first through a grove of subalpine larch, then into a zone of subalpine fir that become shorter as the elevation increases.

The vista to the south encompasses Fairview Mountain, Mt. Aberdeen, The Mitre, and Mt. Lefroy with its impressive ice cap. To the west stretches the long summit ridge of Mt. Victoria. Abbot Pass Hut first comes into sight at the eighth sharp switchback. From then on the panorama unfolds more expansively, eventually taking in the summit of Mt. Temple to the south.

This trail can offer the unusual experience of looking down upon mountain goats: on one occasion I saw two enjoying a siesta on ledges of Mt. Whyte above the teahouse. It's often windy at the end of the established trail, which offers a superlative view over the Lower Victoria Glacier.

Experienced scramblers confident in off-trail travel (see Safety section p. 25) can continue up over scree slopes to a well-defined lateral moraine. A faint path runs along part of its crest; at the end you can traverse toward the edge of a lobe of the Upper Victoria Glacier. **N.B.** Do not venture onto the ice unless properly equipped for glacier travel and familiar with rescue techniques.

The end of the lateral moraine gives a close impression of the crevasses and seracs (ice towers) of the hanging glacier—which are among the features that make negotiating such terrain risky. This proximity also confirms that the thickness of the ice at its edge is approximately 100 m, as improbable as that may seem when looking from the east end of Lake Louise some 6 km away.

This portion of the Upper Victoria Glacier holds historical interest as a location for filming of the 1928 movie "Eternal Love," in which Swiss guide Rudolph Aemmer acted as a double for star John Barrymore.

# Highline between Plain of Six Glaciers and Lake Agnes teahouses

**Distance:** 3.2 km (2.0 mi) — *The Plain of Six Glaciers* trail to Lake Agnes teahouse
**Connector:** 1.5 hours one way
**Elevation gain:** 170 m (560 ft)
**Maximum elevation:** 2120 m (6955 ft)
**Trailhead:** Km 2.2 on *The Plain of Six Glaciers* trail (see p. 34).

0.0 — Sign at junction (elevation 1950 m). Head east, on a contour at first, then climb gradually.

1.3 — Junction (1980 m) with *Shortcut Switchbacks to The Plain of Six Glaciers trail* (see page opposite). Keep straight.

2.0 — Junction (2010 m) with *Highline trail to Big Beehive from Lake Agnes trail* connector (see page opposite). Keep straight.

2.8 — Junction; turn left and climb steadily for Lake Agnes. If wishing to descend to Lake Louise, a more direct route is via the *Lake Agnes* trail (see p. 40) just 100 m ahead on the east side of Mirror Lake.

3.2 — Lake Agnes (2120 m) and teahouse.

This connector trail allows a link of the teahouses at the Plain of Six Glaciers and Lake Agnes without having to descend to Lake Louise. Although the two teahouses are at similar elevations, this trail involves a climb of 170 m since it begins on *The Plain of Six Glaciers* trail below that teahouse. The shortest distance for a trip from Lake Louise taking in the two teahouses [but not the Big Beehive] is 13.3 km (8.2 mi).

The hiking on this trail is straightforward; the highlight is the view from the vicinity of km 1.5 west to the surrounding peaks and over the Lower Victoria Glacier with its well-defined lateral moraines. The trail east of the junction with the direct trail to the Big Beehive winds along steep cliffs, with railings for safety.

The 400 m section at the east end of the trail is steep and narrow, with wooden stairs leading up to Lake Agnes at the finish.

**View across Lake Agnes from near the teahouse to (l to r) Devils Thumb, Mt. Whyte, and Mt. Niblock.**

## Shortcut Switchbacks to The Plain of Six Glaciers trail

**Distance:** 1.0 km (0.6 mi) — *Highline between Plain of Six Glaciers and Lake Agnes teahouses* trail to *The Plain of Six Glaciers* trail
**Connector:** 15—20 minutes one way
**Elevation loss:** 140 m (460 ft)
**Maximum elevation:** 1980 m (6495 ft)
**Trailhead:** Km 1.3 on *Highline between Plain of Six Glaciers and Lake Agnes teahouses* trail (see page opposite).

0.0 — Junction (elevation 1980 m) on the highline trail between the two teahouses. Head steeply downhill.
1.0 — Join *The Plain of Six Glaciers* trail (1840 m) at km 1.4 (see p. 34).

This steep, rocky connector most often comes into play when making a loop from Lake Agnes via the *Highline, The Plain of Six Glaciers,* and the *Lake Louise Lakeshore* trails, without going all the way to the Plain of Six Glaciers teahouse.

## Highline trail to Big Beehive from Lake Agnes trail

**Distance:** 1.0 km (0.6 mi) — *Highline between Plain of Six Glaciers and Lake Agnes teahouses* trail to *Big Beehive from Lake Agnes* trail
**Connector:** 30—40 minutes one way
**Elevation gain:** 250 m (820 ft)
**Maximum elevation:** 2260 m (7415 ft)
**Trailhead:** Km 2.0 on *Highline between Plain of Six Glaciers and Lake Agnes teahouses* trail (see page opposite).

0.0 — Sign at junction (elevation 2010 m). Head northward, climbing steeply.
1.0 — Gain dip in ridge (2260 m) between the Big Beehive and Devils Thumb at km 1.3 of the *Big Beehive from Lake Agnes* trail (see p. 42). Summit of Big Beehive 300 metres to east.

These steep switchbacks give the option to take in the panorama from the summit of the Big Beehive en route to Lake Agnes from the Plain of Six Glaciers. (This is a more strenuous route to Lake Agnes from the Plain of Six Glaciers than by way of the *Highline* trail.)

**Bunchberry.**

# Lake Agnes

See photos p. 38, p. 43, and p. 46.

**Distance:** 3.5 km (2.2 mi) — Lake Louise to Lake Agnes
**Day hike:** 1—1.5 hours one way
**Elevation gain:** 390 m (1280 ft)
**Maximum elevation:** 2120 m (6955 ft)
**Trailhead:** The northeast corner of Lake Louise; pass in front of the Chateau Lake Louise after crossing from the large public parking areas using either of two footbridges over Louise Creek. See the trailhead information for the *Lake Louise Lakeshore* trail (p. 32) for access to Lake Louise.

0.0 — Sign at junction (elevation 1730 m). Take the trail to the right, going up a gradual incline. (The *Lake Louise Lakeshore* trail (p. 32) keeps straight.)

0.2 — Pavement ends. Keep straight, crossing the horse trail to the Plain of Six Glaciers. Begin steady climb on a constant grade.

1.6 — Switchback in an avalanche gully (1920 m).

2.4 — Junction with horse trail. Keep left.

2.7 — Junction at Mirror Lake (2030 m). Turn right along trail that starts 10 m back from lake and begin switchbacks. (Trail to left connects in 100 m with *Highline between Plain of Six Glaciers and Lake Agnes teahouses* (see p. 38) at km 2.8.)

3.2 — Junction (2080 m) with direct route to the Little Beehive: this 400 m connector joins the *Little Beehive from Lake Agnes* trail (see p. 46) at km 0.3—thus saving 200 m if the Little Beehive is the first objective. Keep straight for Lake Agnes.

3.5 — Lake Agnes (2120 m) and teahouse, at top of wooden stairs beside waterfall.

The steadily climbing but deservedly popular trail to Lake Agnes leads to a mesmerizing body of water set in a wild, steep-walled cirque.

The trail travels through subalpine forest, whose two main tree species are recognizable by examining their needles. Those of the subalpine fir are two-sided, with rounded ends; using alliteration, think of "flat, friendly fir." The needles of Engelmann spruce (named after a botanist) are four-sided, with sharp-pointed ends—thus "square, spiny spruce." The bark of these trees also helps in identification: subalpine fir has smooth grey bark with bubbles of sap underneath, whereas Engelmann spruce has rough, corrugated bark.

The opening reached at km 1.6 is the result of winter avalanche activity. It grants a vista across to Fairview Mountain, on whose summit people who have scrambled to the top may be visible (see *Fairview Mountain* description, p. 51). The km 1.6 vantage point also allows views down to Lake Louise with its typically turquoise colour. The apparent miniaturization of any canoes upon the lake reinforces the fact that almost half of the elevation gain to Lake Agnes has been covered.

The trail doubles back from the first switchback, then curves around to the junction with the horse trail from Lake Louise. (Although the distance back to the Chateau is less by the horse trail, I recommend sticking to the footpath since its grade is gentler and easier on the knees for descent.)

Mirror Lake lies 300 m beyond the horse trail junction. This body of water is

**Looking east from west end of Lake Agnes, showing teahouse.**

small in size but has a spectacular setting with the near-vertical east face of the Big Beehive rising above it. The cliff's horizontal layers, which give this feature its name, show the sedimentary origin of the Canadian Rockies. The entire range is made of rock laid down particle-by-particle in the sea that once submerged this area. The rock was then uplifted, folded, and fractured by powerful forces during a long period of mountain building.

The story of the origin of the name of Lake Agnes is an interesting one. Lady Agnes Macdonald first visited the area in 1886 with her husband Sir John A., first Prime Minister of Canada. (They travelled on a Canadian Pacific Railway steam locomotive, on which Lady Agnes took the exciting method of sitting up front on the cowcatcher.) On a later trip she walked up to the lake, led by Willoughby Astley, first manager of the Lake Louise Chalet (1890-1894). Lake Agnes was then known as one of the "Lakes in the Clouds," the other being present-day Mirror Lake.

As it happened, Mr. Astley had led Agnes Knox, a "Toronto elocutionist," to the lake just a few days earlier. He relates: "Now we were in a fix, as Lady Macdonald understood from high C.P.R. officialdom that she was the first woman to be shown those lakes." By chance, the first names of the two women coincided, and both seem to have been satisfied with sharing the honour of having the lake in their name.

A popular full-day hike links the Lake Agnes teahouse with the Plain of Six Glaciers teahouse via the *Highline* connector (see p. 38). The shortest distance for a trip from Lake Louise taking in the two teahouses [but not the Big Beehive] is 13.3 km (8.2 mi).

# Big Beehive from Lake Agnes

See photo p. 46 and fourth colour photo starting opposite p. 64.

**Distance:** 1.6 km (1.0 mi) — Lake Agnes to the Big Beehive
**Extension of day hike:** 45 minutes one way
**Elevation gain:** 150 m (490 ft)
**Maximum elevation:** 2270 m (7445 ft)
**Trailhead:** Lake Agnes teahouse (see two previous pages).

0.0 — Lake Agnes teahouse (elevation 2120 m). Proceed on the trail along the north shore of Lake Agnes.

0.7 — West end of Lake Agnes. Continue around the end of the lake and begin ascending steep switchbacks above the southwest corner of the lake.

1.3 — Gain ridge (2260 m) between the Big Beehive and Devils Thumb. Turn left along generally level section; straight ahead is the *Highline trail to Big Beehive from Lake Agnes trail* connector (see p. 39). Descend slightly at the end of the trail.

1.6 — Big Beehive shelter (2270 m).

Although the Big Beehive looms above the teahouse at the east end of Lake Agnes, the ascent is not as daunting as it might appear. It involves an elevation gain of 150 m, true, yet well-graded switchbacks ease the climb.

The initial 700 m of this energetic extension of the day hike to Lake Agnes are mainly level, providing a pleasant saunter if that is enough at this point. Along this stretch there is a good chance of sighting a pika (I pronounce it pee-ka, although pie-ka is also heard). This small greyish-brown mammal has rounded ears and a vestigal tailbone. It is also known as the "rock rabbit," and is related to rabbits and hares.

Pikas give a high-pitched "eek" alarm call that I think of as the "squeak-a of a pika." These residents of high elevation rocky areas adjacent to vegetated slopes gather flowers and stalks in late summer and early fall, depositing them into haypile-shaped

**Talus cone below the north face of Fairview Mountain, as seen from the Big Beehive.**

**Big Beehive (note gazebo on top of cliff) and Lake Agnes from *Little Beehive from Lake Agnes* trail.**

caches. Pikas are active year-round, relying primarily on these stashes of sun-dried food over the winter. However, they do move about in tunnels under the snow and can supplement their diet with lichens found on rocks.

Once up the steady switchbacks to the ridge between the Big Beehive and Devils Thumb, it is but 300 m to the end of the trail just below the true high point. The red-roofed gazebo here, which is visible from the east end of Lake Louise, gives an unusual perspective upon the lake from 540 m (1770 ft) above.

Clark's nutcrackers often frequent this spot and the Lake Agnes teahouse because of the number of people present. However, these birds are not at all in need of a handout. Their long, chisel-like bills are very efficient in extracting seeds from cones, and prevent getting pitch on their facial feathers in the process.

The Clark's' nutcracker is named after Capt. William Clark of the Lewis and Clark Expedition to the western United States (1805-1806), which provided the first description of the species. (The Lewis' woodpecker—found occasionally in Banff National Park—owes its name to Merriwether Lewis, the other leader of the expedition.)

Clark's nutcrackers—I fondly call them "Clarkies"—have great success at recovering the seeds they store in small holes made with their sturdy bills. These food reserves are usually situated on windswept ridges that stay clear of snow. This helps in relocation; furthermore, nutcrackers have excellent spatial memory, finding seeds they may have stored months earlier, using cues from nearby objects such as stones. This capability gives Clark's nutcrackers an important advantage in that with reliable energy supplies they can have their young early in the year. This gives their offspring a better chance of survival since they have more time to put on weight and to learn the strategies of nutcracker life before winter arrives.

# Goat Pass

**Distance:** 1.0 km (0.6 mi) — West end of Lake Agnes to Goat Pass
**Off-trail scramble:** 1—1.5 hour(s) one way
**Elevation gain:** 310 m (1015 ft)
**Maximum elevation:** 2430 m (7970 ft)
**Trailhead:** Km 0.7 on *Big Beehive from Lake Agnes* trail (see two previous pages).

0.0 — Head west from the west end of Lake Agnes (elevation 2120 m) toward the head of the cirque between Mt. Whyte and Mt. Niblock, taking a path along the base of the south aspect of Mt. St. Piran.
0.5 — Begin bearing north (right) to reach the pass, situated between Mt. Niblock and Mt. St. Piran, preferably on a rough path.
1.0 — Goat Pass (2430 m).

Dedicated off-trail scrambling enthusiasts can use this approach to Goat Pass, the local name for the saddle between Mt. Niblock and Mt. St. Piran. It is an appropriate name since mountain goats are often found in the vicinity. On one visit here I enjoyed watching a nanny goat and her kid, the latter appearing precocious and vulnerable by turns. I was able to get some favourite photographic images by freezing in place while the animals went about their routine.

Another approach to Goat Pass is to take the established route to the summit of Mt. St. Piran (see p. 47). Then descend its southwest ridge to the pass, after which Lake Agnes can be reached by taking this route in reverse.

Access to Goat Pass is also possible from Minewakun Lake (see p. 56). (The pass was originally named Minewakun Pass by Samuel Allen.)

**Mountain goat nanny and kid.**

# Devils Thumb

See photos pages 2-3, p. 38, and next page.

**Distance:** 1.1 km (0.7 mi) — *Big Beehive from Lake Agnes* trail to summit of Devils Thumb

**Off-trail scramble:** 1 hour one way
**Elevation gain:** 198 m (649 ft)
**Maximum elevation:** 2458 m (8062 ft)
**Trailhead:** Km 1.3 on *Big Beehive from Lake Agnes* trail (see p. 42). [This is also the end of the *Highline trail to Big Beehive from Lake Agnes trail* connector at km 1.0 (see p. 39).]

0.0 — Sign at junction (elevation 2260 m); take less-travelled path to the west.

0.1 — Ignore the first faint path to the left, then take the second path to the left. **N.B.** Do not venture up to the right, which leads to rockclimbing terrain on the east face of Devils Thumb. Travel beneath the south cliffs, more or less on a contour.

0.6 — Head right up the prominent gully, climbing steeply up the rocky slope, aiming for the low point on the ridge between Devils Thumb and Mt. Whyte.

0.9 — Gain the low point on the ridge; turn right and continue climbing.

1.1 — Summit of Devils Thumb (2458 m).

The ascent of Devils Thumb entails off-trail scrambling; the reward for such effort is a dizzying bird's-eye view of Lake Agnes. There is a cluster of tall stone cairns at the summit, which from below could be mistaken for a group of people.

The very top of Devils Thumb is surprisingly flat: a fair-sized plateau of rock split by deep fractures, giving it the look of a gigantic natural cobblestone avenue. On a visit early one June I found alpine wildflowers such as moss campion and purple saxifrage already in bloom—an illustration of their hardiness, to be out so early in such a high, cool, windy place.

**The author on the summit plateau of Devils Thumb; Slate Range on left skyline.**

# Little Beehive from Lake Agnes

**Distance:** 0.9 km (0.6 mi) — Lake Agnes teahouse to the Little Beehive
**Extension of day hike:** 45 minutes one way
**Elevation gain:** 105 m (345 ft)
**Maximum elevation:** 2225 m (7300 ft)
**Trailhead:** Lake Agnes teahouse (see p. 40).

0.0 — Lake Agnes teahouse (elevation 2120 m). Take trail leading along north shore of Lake Agnes for just 15 m, then turn sharply right up steady incline (past outhouses).

0.3 — Keep straight at the junction with the direct route to the Little Beehive from km 3.2 of the *Lake Agnes* trail (see p. 40).

0.6 — Keep straight at the junction (2175 m) with the start of the *Mt. St. Piran* trail (see page opposite). Descend slightly near the end of the trail.

0.9 — Site of former fire lookout on the Little Beehive (2225 m).

The ascent of the Little Beehive provides an attractive alternative if eager to do more hiking from Lake Agnes but not desirous of tackling the greater climb to the Big Beehive. The summit of the Little Beehive is the former location of a fire lookout (see interpretive signage on site)...all that now remains is the foundation. For more information, refer to the author's book **Fire Lookout Hikes in the Canadian Rockies**, also published by Luminous Compositions. As is the case with the places chosen for all fire lookouts, the Little Beehive grants a superb panorama.

A bonus of the Little Beehive compared with its higher cousin is the view north up the Bow Valley including Mt. Hector and the deep blue waters of Hector Lake. Another extra might be the sight of a golden eagle soaring by the cliffs of the Little Beehive, riding the wind currents on huge outstretched wings.

**View from the *Little Beehive from Lake Agnes* trail: (l to r) Mt. Aberdeen, Mt. Lefroy with the Big Beehive below, Mt. Victoria, and Devils Thumb with Lake Agnes below.**

# Mt. St. Piran

See photo p. 122.

**Distance:** 1.6 km (1.0 mi) — *Little Beehive from Lake Agnes* trail to summit of
Mt. St. Piran
**Extension of day hike and off-trail scramble:** 1.5 hours one way
**Elevation gain:** 475 m (1560 ft)
**Maximum elevation:** 2650 m (8692 ft)
**Trailhead:** Km 0.6 on *Little Beehive from Lake Agnes* trail (see page opposite).

0.0 — Junction (elevation 2175 m) on *Little Beehive from Lake Agnes* trail. Veer left onto a faint trail that climbs through a subalpine larch forest before settling into a series of switchbacks up the southeast aspect of Mt. St. Piran.

1.3 — The defined trail fades after reaching a dip on the northeast ridge. Continue to the summit by turning left and scrambling over rocks.

1.6 — Summit of Mt. St. Piran (2650 m).

The hike and off-trail scramble up Mt. St. Piran is a favourite in the Lake Louise area. The peak is named after the hometown in Cornwall, England, of Willoughby Astley, first manager of the original Lake Louise Chalet. The rather faint but nicely graded switchbacking trail up the southeastern aspect was built by Swiss guides in the early 1900s.

There is a good chance of seeing a pika at the top of Mt. St. Piran. Once when I was quiet and patient one approached me (out of curiosity; rest assured I did not feed it) and eventually began licking the runners I was wearing, which had gotten wet in fresh snow on the way up. Living in an often dry environment, it took advantage of the opportunity to get water, and I was able to get photographs with it filling the frame—with a normal 50 mm lens on my camera! I laughingly refer to the close-up images I took as "The Attack of the Killer Pika."

Travelling off-trail for some 600 m down along the southwest ridge from the summit of Mt. St. Piran leads to the col between it and Mt. Niblock, known locally as Goat Pass. From the pass it is possible to descend into the cirque to the south and connect with the trail at the west end of Lake Agnes by doing the off-trail route described on p. 44 in reverse.

**Pika photographed on the
summit of Mt. St. Piran.**

# Saddleback

**Distance:** 3.7 km (2.3 mi) — Lake Louise to Saddleback
**Day hike:** 1.5—2 hours one way
**Elevation gain:** 600 m (1970 ft)
**Maximum elevation:** 2330 m (7642 ft)
**Trailhead:** The southeast corner of Lake Louise, near the boathouse. A short connector links the west end of the upper parking lots with this trail at km 0.1.

0.0 — Sign (elevation 1730 m). Keep straight.
0.1 — Junction with short connector coming in on left from the upper parking lots. Keep straight.
0.3 — Junction (1775 m) with *Fairview Lookout* trail (see page opposite). Keep straight.
0.4 — Junction with *Paradise Creek from Lake Louise* trail (see p. 57). Keep right.
1.1 — Wide avalanche swath. Switchbacks begin on far side.
2.2 — Junction. Main trail continues straight; shorter but steeper route climbs up to right.
2.6 — Junction with steeper route up from km 2.2 junction. Keep left and continue climbing, more gradually, until a final series of switchbacks that starts 400 m before reaching open meadows below the pass.
3.5 — Gain crest; continue 200 m straight ahead to height of pass.
3.7 — Saddleback (2330 m).

The Saddleback is the name for the dip between Saddle Mountain and Fairview Mountain. The trail to it skirts the east cliffs of Fairview Mountain, rising steadily through larch-sprinkled avalanche slopes that allow good views of the Bow Valley. After the km 2.6 junction, more, and bigger, subalpine larches appear: truly eye-catching in their golden autumn raiment.

The crest reached at km 3.5 was once the site of a third teahouse in the Lake Louise area (in addition to those still extant at the Plain of Six Glaciers and Lake Agnes). The Saddleback teahouse, operated by the Canadian Pacific Railway, opened in 1922. The lease was cancelled in 1937, after which the teahouse was demolished.

**The author just below the km 3.5 crest on the *Saddleback* trail; Mt. Temple beyond.**

# Fairview Lookout

**Distance:** 0.7 km (0.4 mi) — *Saddleback* trail to lookout
**Day hike:** 30 minutes one way
**Elevation gain:** 100 m (330 ft)
**Maximum elevation:** 1875 m (6150 ft)
**Trailhead:** Km 0.3 on *Saddleback* trail (see page opposite).

0.0 — Sign  at junction (elevation 1775 m). Turn right for Fairview Lookout.
0.7 — Fairview Lookout (1875 m).

"The lake seemed like a great basin filled with liquid under magic spell, where the quietly changing sunbeams resembled an enchanter's wand, which at the lightest touch produced wonderful colorings and weird effects in the uncertain light." This evocative passage in Walter Wilcox's 1909 book **The Rockies of Canada** gives an impression of what the Fairview Lookout can reveal.

This platform 100 m above the south side of Lake Louise is not readily visible from below; therefore this trail is much less visited than the *Lake Louise Lakeshore* trail on the opposite shore. It can thus offer the opportunity for quiet contemplation of the magnificent surroundings. It also gives a fine view of the Chateau Lake Louise.

The usual return is by reversing the trail. However, it is possible to take a rough path, 1.4 km (0.9 mi) long, that descends steeply to Lake Louise and follows the often boggy south shore back to the boathouse.

**Chateau Lake Louise and Lower Pipestone Valley from Fairview Lookout (1986 photograph).**

# Saddle Mountain

See photo p. 128.

**Distance:** 0.5 km (0.3 mi) — Saddleback to summit of Saddle Mountain
**Off-trail scramble:** 20—30 minutes one way
**Elevation gain:** 90 m (295 ft)
**Maximum elevation:** 2420 m (7938 ft)
**Trailhead:** The high point on the Saddleback (see p. 48).

0.0 — The Saddleback (elevation 2330 m). Take faint path to south (left as coming from Lake Louise) through subalpine larches on northwest ridge of Saddle Mountain. The path leads into the open, continuing beyond which requires navigating over and around large boulders.
0.5 — Summit of Saddle Mountain (2420 m).

It's an easy scramble from the Saddleback up the northwest ridge of Saddle Mountain, so named because of the shape of its two peaks. The summit on the west peak lies at the edge of a precipitous drop-off to Paradise Valley, with views of Paradise Creek and Lake Annette. It also represents an excellent vantage point to marvel at the spectacular north face of Mt. Temple with its glaciated cap.

Below and to the east of Mt. Temple is the outlier known as 'Little Temple,' another feature with twin summits. Its ascent, which is another off-trail scramble (see p. 89), gives a reciprocal view back to Saddle Mountain with its southern cliffs—impressive even if they don't match those of Mt. Temple.

**The author's wife Jane on the summit of Saddle Mountain, looking over Paradise Valley to Mt. Temple.**

# Fairview Mountain

See photos p. 5 and p. 119.

**Distance:** 1.3 km (0.8 mi) — Saddleback to summit of Fairview Mountain
**Extension of day hike:** 1—1.5 hour(s) one way
**Elevation gain:** 414 m (1358 ft)
**Maximum elevation:** 2744 m (9000 ft)
**Trailhead:** The high point on the Saddleback (see p. 48).

0.0 — The Saddleback (elevation 2330 m). Take the path to north (right as coming from Lake Louise), initially through subalpine larches, then up steep switchbacks on the southeast aspect of Fairview Mountain.
1.3 — Summit of Fairview Mountain (2744 m).

People wanting to ascend Fairview Mountain sometimes head up the scree slope immediately apparent from the crest at km 3.5 of the *Saddleback* trail. However, it is much preferable to take the switchbacking trail up the southeastern aspect of the mountain, starting from the high point of the Saddleback at km 3.7.

The summit of Fairview Mountain lives up to its name due to an elevation of 2744 m. One of the highlights of attaining the top is the view down to Lake Louise, more than a vertical kilometre below.

(cont. next page)

**The author looking from the summit of Fairview Mountain over the Upper Victoria Glacier and Lower Victoria Glacier, with *The Plain of Six Glaciers* trail visible.**

(Cont. from previous page)

This vantage point gives an excellent appreciation of the delta forming at the west end of Lake Louise. The glaciers up-valley scrape off material as rocks embedded within the ice gouge against underlying bedrock. This sediment is carried down by turbid Louise Creek; when the creek reaches the relatively still waters of the lake, the heavier particles settle out. The colour difference in the water where this takes place is apparent. Ever so slowly, this process is filling in Lake Louise, whose maximum depth is presently 70 m (230 ft).

The lighter particles in the sediment, so fine that they are referred to as 'rock flour,' remain in suspension. They are responsible for the characteristic turquoise shade of glacier-fed lakes, since sunlight reflecting off them carries wavelengths of the blue-green portion of the visible spectrum to our eyes.

Fairview Mountain gives an impressive vista over the glaciated valley of the Plain of Six Glaciers above Lake Louise, and of the surrounding peaks including mts. Aberdeen, Lefroy, Victoria, and Whyte. The network of trails in the vicinity is laid out below, among them those near Lake Agnes that connect Mirror Lake, the Big Beehive, the Little Beehive, and Mt. St. Piran.

Fairview Mountain grants other panoramas as well: to the north—Bow and Cirque peaks, Dolomite Mountain, and Mt. Hector; to the northeast—Molar Mountain and the Pipestone Valley; to the east—the peaks around Skoki Valley, and Protection Mountain with its long ridge; and to the south—the landmarks of Castle and Pilot mountains. It is well worthwhile staying on the summit to enjoy these scenic gems, though lingering long will often call for those extra layers due to a cool breeze.

Return the same way. Do not try to return to Lake Louise by descending to the north, a vain attempt which will only lead to having to climb back up, if not having to be unnecessarily rescued.

**View west from the summit of Fairview Mountain to (l to r) Haddo Peak, Mt. Aberdeen, Mt. Lefroy, and part of Mt. Victoria.**

# Sheol Valley

See photo next page.

**Distance:** 4.1 km (2.5 mi) — Saddleback to Paradise Creek
**Extension to day hike:** 1—1.5 hour(s) one way
**Elevation loss:** 475 m (1560 ft)
**Maximum elevation:** 2330 m (7642 ft)
**Trailhead:** The high point of the Saddleback (see p. 48). **N.B.** This trail is subject to closure or voluntary restrictions (e.g., minimum party size) due to its location in grizzly bear habitat.

0.0 — The Saddleback (elevation 2330 m). Head west (straight ahead when coming from Lake Louise) and drop down a series of steep switchbacks.
4.1 — Junction (1855 m) with Paradise Creek at km 4.2 of *Paradise Valley* trail (see p. 60).

This trail allows a long circuit to Lake Louise rather than returning back down the *Saddleback* trail. The descent through Sheol Valley passes close to the sheer east cliffs of Sheol Mountain.

Explorer/mountaineer Samuel Allen gave the mountain its name. The peak seemed to him reminiscent of the 'abode of the dead' in Hebrew legend—a rather morbid observation, sadly presaging Allen's later mental breakdown. The valley is actually a vibrant oasis of wildflowers during summer's prime.

The initial section of this trail from the Saddleback is through a dense stand of subalpine larch, which have an intriguing aura when the fresh, soft, green needles of summer push forth from nodes on the long branches. Lower down the trail can be found rough-barked Engelmann spruce. This species is also coniferous, although in the more usual scenario it does not shed its needles all at once like the subalpine larch.

Engelmann spruce is subject to natural utilization by two species of woodpecker, the black-backed and the three-toed, which deploy an unusual strategy to forage on these trees. Rather than drilling in like species such as the downy and hairy woodpeckers, these two species (in which the males have yellow on their heads) hit the trunk with sideways strikes. This flicks off flakes of bark, exposing insects and larvae upon which to feed. The pieces of bark can be seen around the base of the tree, and the missing pieces leave a pattern of lighter patches on the trunk.

From the junction at Paradise Creek, the loop proceeds downstream to the junction at km 1.3 of the *Paradise Valley* trail (see p. 60), then takes the *Paradise Creek from Lake Louise* trail in reverse to the description on p. 57. The total distance for the circuit is 14.9 km (9.2 mi). A shorter option, preferably with transportation arranged, is to go out to the Moraine Lake Road from the km 1.3 junction on the *Paradise Valley* trail.

**Hiker Marty Campbell on the *Sheol Valley* trail.**

# Ross Lake, Yoho National Park, from Lake Louise

**Distance:** 7.4 km (4.6 mi) — Lake Louise to Ross Lake
**Day hike:** 2 hours one way
**Elevation gain:** None overall, although the trail undulates gently
**Maximum elevation:** 1755 m (5755 ft)
**Trailhead:** The northeast corner of Lake Louise; pass in front of the Chateau Lake Louise after crossing from the large public parking areas using either of two foot-bridges over Louise Creek (see p. 32). **N.B.** This trail is currently open to mountain biking.

0.0 — Junction (elevation 1740 m). Rather than taking either the *Lake Louise Lakeshore* or *Lake Agnes* trails, follow a service road that heads toward the northwest corner of the Chateau Lake Louise.

0.1 — At the northwest corner of the Chateau Lake Louise, head north about 20 m to pick up a trail going uphill to the right through trees.

0.3 — Keep left uphill just before the west end of the parking area for the 'Hillside Cottage' staff residence.

0.4 — Sign at actual start of this trail (used by horse parties for the first 100 m).

0.5 — Keep right where horse trail goes left.

3.6 — Cross creek (1740 m). Keep straight; path to *Minewakun Lake* (see next page) climbs to left just before creek.

6.0 — Cross boulder-filled bed of Divide Creek. Optional off-trail descent down creek bed to Great Divide Exhibit on former Highway 1A.

6.2 — Signs at Banff National Park/Yoho National Park boundary.

7.4 — Ross Lake (1740 m). Options from here include taking the 1.3 km (0.8 mi) trail (mountain bikers must walk this) down to the former Highway 1A and then heading back to Lake Louise Drive in 9.2 km (5.7 mi) or heading west 1.8 km (1.1 mi) to the access road for the Lake O'Hara trailhead (the former Hwy 1A is open to mountain biking). Another possibility is to continue west on trail from Ross Lake to the limited access Lake O'Hara Road. Then head right down the road to the Lake O'Hara trailhead parking area or left up to Lake O'Hara. (Neither this trail or the Lake O'Hara Road are open to mountain biking.)

This trail occasionally passes through avalanche gullies from the Little Bee-hive, Mt. St. Piran, and Mt. Niblock, which permit views east and (later) north. Otherwise it stays in subalpine forest, home to such bird species as dark-eyed junco, hermit thrush, and three-toed woodpecker.

The narrow gorge of the creek that drains Minewakun Lake serves as a landmark along the way. (See the next page for access to that tiny tarn.)

An option that stays within Banff National Park is to bushwhack for about 700 m down the boulder-and-log filled bed of Divide Creek. (This is often dry late in the season, but is no place to be during heavy rain.)

This trail to Ross Lake from Lake Louise was built before Highway 1A, which parallels it and which has been closed to vehicles and is also now a route for self-propelled recreation.

# Minewakun Lake

**Distance:** 1.0 km (0.6 mi) — *Ross Lake, Yoho National Park, from Lake Louise* trail to Minewakun Lake
**Extension to day hike:** 30—40 minutes one way
**Elevation gain:** 290 m (950 ft)
**Maximum elevation:** 2030 m (6660 ft)
**Trailhead:** Km 3.6 on *Ross Lake, Yoho National Park, from Lake Louise* trail (see previous page).

0.0 — Junction (elevation 1740 m) just before creek flowing from Minewakun Lake. Turn left up steep path beside narrow gorge.
1.0 — Minewakun Lake (2030 m).

This narrow, steep path gives access to tiny, little-known Minewakun Lake—not to be confused with very popular and much larger Lake Minnewanka near Banff townsite. The summit of Mt. St. Piran (see p. 47) reveals this little gem tucked away in the small valley between that mountain and the northeast ridge of Mt. Niblock.

{A very rough shortcut, 300 m long, follows the creek from what was a small parking area on the north side of Highway 1A [closed to vehicles but open to hikers and mountain bikers], 4.0 km (2.5 mi) from the intersection with Lake Louise Drive. This steep path joins the trail described above at the trail-head.}

An interesting off-trail option from Minewakun Lake is to climb to Goat Pass, about 1.6 km (1.0 mi) from the lake. The route first follows the course of the stream that feeds the lake, then turns south (left) to begin the steep ascent to the pass, 400 m (1310 ft) higher than the tarn. **N.B.** Snow lingers on the sheltered north side of the pass late into summer, so an ice axe is recommended in case self-arrest becomes necessary.

Descent can be made to Lake Agnes: see the *Goat Pass* description, p. 44. Or, if still full of energy, tackle the ascent of Mt. St. Piran (see p. 47)—the summit grants the aforementioned view of this seldom-visited lake.

**Unusual rocks on the outlet creek near Lake Minewakun.**

# Paradise Creek from Lake Louise

**Distance:** 3.8 km (2.4 mi) — *Saddleback* trail to *Paradise Valley* trail
**Day hike:** 45 minutes—1 hour one way
**Elevation gain:** 50 m (165 ft)
**Maximum elevation:** 1825 m (5985 ft)
**Trailhead:** Km 0.4 on *Saddleback* trail (see p. 48).

0.0 — Junction (elevation 1775 m). Keep left; *Saddleback* trail to right.
3.8 — Junction (1825 m) with *Paradise Valley* trail at km 1.3 (see p. 60). The foot-bridge over Paradise Creek itself is 300 m ahead, 100 m beyond the km 1.1 junction on the *Paradise Valley* trail.

      This is a straightforward route through forest. It can be used as part of a circuit over the Saddleback, down through Sheol Valley, along Paradise Creek, and back to Lake Louise (see p. 53).

Mule deer buck.

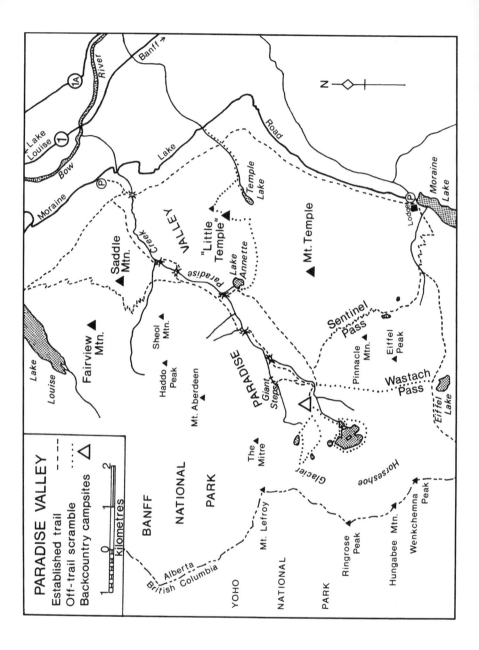

PARADISE VALLEY

Established trail — — —
Off-trail scramble ........
Backcountry campsites △

kilometres
0 1 2

BANFF

NATIONAL

PARK

YOHO

NATIONAL

PARK

Alberta
British Columbia

1A

River

Banff ↗

Lake
Louise

1

Bow

Moraine

P

Lake

Road

Temple
Lake

Moraine
Lake

Lodge P

Saddle
Mtn.

Creek

VALLEY

"Little"
Temple

Lake
Annette

Paradise

Mt. Temple

Sentinel
Pass

Eiffel
Peak

Fairview
Mtn.

Lake

Louise

Sheol
Mtn.

Haddo
Peak

Mt. Aberdeen

PARADISE

Giant
Steps

Pinnacle
Mtn.

Wastach
Pass

Eiffel
Lake

The
Mitre

Glacier

Horseshoe

Mt. Lefroy

Ringrose
Peak

Hungabee Mtn.

Wenkchemna
Peak

# Paradise Valley

**The author crossing bridge at km 3.9 on *Paradise Valley* trail; Sheol Mountain ahead.**

# Paradise Valley

See photos p. 8, p. 50, p. 59, p. 65, and sixth colour photo starting opposite p. 64.

**Distance:** 9.0 km (5.6 mi) — Moraine Lake Road to Paradise Valley backcountry campground

**Day hike or backpack:** 2—2.5 hours one way

**Elevation gain:** 370 m (1215 ft)

**Maximum elevation:** 2090 m (6855 ft)

**Trailhead:** Parking area 2.5 km (1.6 mi) along Moraine Lake Road, on the west side (the right side as coming from Lake Louise). The Moraine Lake Road begins 3.0 km (1.9 mi) from Lake Louise Village along Lake Louise Drive (see trailhead info for *Lake Louise Lakeshore* trail, p. 32). [Moraine Lake Road is closed in winter— roughly October to May.] **N.B.** This trail is subject to closure or voluntary restrictions (e.g., minimum party size) due to its location in grizzly bear habitat. Also note that there is no mountain biking beyond the first 1.1 km of this trail.

0.0 — Parking area (elevation 1720 m). Start up short steep section.

0.4 — Keep left at junction with mountain bike and cross-country ski trail that comes in on the right; travel parallel to Paradise Creek.

1.1 — Keep right at junction (1800 m) with *Paradise Creek from Moraine Lake* trail (see p. 88); first (lowest) footbridge over Paradise Creek 100 m to left.

1.3 — Turn left at junction with *Paradise Creek from Lake Louise* trail (see p. 57).

3.3 — Cross second footbridge over Paradise Creek (first one met on this trail) to south side of creek

3.9 — Cross back over to north side of Paradise Creek on third footbridge.

4.2 — Keep straight at junction (1855 m) with *Sheol Valley* trail (see p. 53).

5.1 — Keep straight at junction (1900 m) with *Lake Annette and Paradise Valley Highline* trail (see p. 62).

6.8 — Cross fourth footbridge over Paradise Creek.

7.2 — Cross fifth footbridge over Paradise Creek. Keep straight at the junction just beyond with a faint path (not recommended) that leads to the Giant Steps. Begin to climb more steeply beside a small gorge.

8.2 — Keep left at junction (2070 m) with *Giant Steps* trail (see p. 63).

8.5 — Keep left at junction with connector trail to Giant Steps.

8.7 — Keep right at junction (2080 m) with *Sentinel Pass from Paradise Valley* trail (see p. 64).

9.0 — Paradise Valley backcountry campground (2090 m).

The first views on the *Paradise Valley* trail come at the footbridge at km 3.3. The twin peaks of Saddle Mountain are due north, the cliffs of Sheol Mountain are ahead to the west, while to the south soars the dauntingly steep 1200 m north face of ice-capped Mt. Temple.

Shortly after crossing back to the north side of the creek lies the junction for Sheol Valley and the Saddleback. Another 900 m sees arrival at the junction with the *Lake Annette and Paradise Valley Highline* trail, after which the trail passes through a number of avalanche slopes. These grant neck-craning views of Mt. Aberdeen (named after Lord Aberdeen, Governor General of Canada in the late 1800s) and slightly lower

Haddo Peak (named after the eldest son of Lord Aberdeen, George, Lord Haddo).

The spur trail to the popular Giant Steps waterfalls veers off at km 8.2, then shortly after the junction with the *Sentinel Pass from Paradise Valley* trail lies the end of this trail. This is the site of the Paradise Valley backcountry campground, the only such facility in the three main valleys close to Lake Louise. Because of the possibility of closures due to bear activity, reservations for these backcountry campsites can be made no more than 24 hours in advance.

There are many Columbian ground squirrels in the meadows at the head of the valley, below the moraines of the Horseshoe Glacier. These small mammals issue a high-pitched call if alarmed, and dive into their burrows.

**Columbian ground squirrel.**

The subalpine forest of this valley is frequented by another mammal—one with quills—so I think of it as Paradise for porcupines! Despite their protective adaptation, porcupines don't represent a threat to people (see p. 82). But don't leave gear, including boots and packs, unattended, as these animals love to gnaw on most anything with salt content.

An attractive choice on leaving the head of Paradise Valley is to make a partial loop by taking the first 600 m of the *Sentinel Pass from Paradise Valley* trail, then the *Lake Annette and Paradise Valley Highline* trail in the opposite direction to the description on the next page. The distance this way back to Moraine Lake Road, including taking in the Giant Steps waterfalls (see p. 63), is 19.9 km (12.3 mi). Yes, this makes for a full day, but it doesn't add much to the trip that simply goes back the same way plus detours to the Giant Steps: only 0.7 km (0.4 mi) distance and 40 m (130 ft) elevation gain.

The name of Paradise Valley, although it sounds generic, came about in an unusual manner. The valley was discovered by Walter Wilcox and his mountaineering companions in 1894, not by heading up from the Bow Valley, but by the rather more strenuous approach from Lake Louise via Mitre Col between Mt. Lefroy and Mt. Aberdeen. The party enjoyed a 500 m bum-slide down to the valley, which they found enchanting after having travelled among "high mountains covered with glaciers and snow and altogether devoid of vegetation."

# Lake Annette and Paradise Valley Highline

**Distance:** 3.7 km (2.3 mi) — *Paradise Valley* trail to *Sentinel Pass from Paradise Valley* trail
**Extension to day hike:** 1 hour one way
**Elevation gain:** 210 m (690 ft)
**Maximum elevation:** 2120 m (6955 ft)
**Trailhead:** Km 5.1 on *Paradise Valley* trail (see p. 60). **N.B.** This trail and the *Paradise Valley* trail are subject to closure or voluntary restrictions (e.g., minimum party size) due to their location in grizzly bear habitat.

0.0 — Sign at junction (elevation 1900 m). Turn left.

0.2 — Cross footbridge over Paradise Creek and begin climbing.

0.6 — Lake Annette (1965 m). The trail along the upper south side of Paradise Valley goes right and climbs through stands of subalpine fir and subalpine larch.

3.7 — Junction (2110 m) with *Sentinel Pass from Paradise Valley* trail (see p. 64) at km 0.6.

This optional extension to the *Paradise Valley* trail leads to a tarn—a body of water filling a glacially scooped basin—set directly beneath the impressive north face of the highest peak in the Lake Louise area, Mt. Temple (3543 m). Lake Annette's name commemorates the mother of Willoughby Astley, first manager of the original Lake Louise Chalet.

A scenic highline route continues from the lake on the south side of the valley, above Paradise Creek, to reach the *Sentinel Pass from Paradise Valley* trail. Here there are two choices. The more popular one is to turn right to connect with the main *Paradise Valley* trail via a portion of the *Sentinel Pass from Paradise Valley* trail, thus making the circuit mentioned at the bottom of the previous page.

The other possibility is to climb left to Sentinel Pass, at which point the most likely scenario is to descend its south side (see *Sentinel Pass from Larch Valley*, p. 74).

**Lake Annette.**

# Giant Steps

**Distance:** 0.6 km (0.4 mi) — *Paradise Valley* trail to waterfalls
**Extension to day hike:** 20—25 minutes one way
**Elevation loss:** 60 m (195 ft)
**Maximum elevation:** 2070 m (6790 ft)
**Trailhead:** Km 8.2 on *Paradise Valley* trail (see p. 60). **N.B.** This trail and the *Paradise Valley* trail are subject to closure or voluntary restrictions (e.g., minimum party size) due to their location in grizzly bear habitat.

0.0 — Sign at junction (elevation 2070 m). Turn right.
0.2 — Keep right at junction with connector that goes left to join the *Paradise Valley* trail at km 8.5.
0.6 — Giant Steps (2010 m).

The Giant Steps, a series of waterfalls where a tributary stream of Paradise Creek cascades over thick step-like beds of flat-lying quartzite, are a deserving attraction in Paradise Valley. A day hike to visit them is a good outing for the long days falling close to the June 21st summer solstice since it involves 17.6 km (10.9 mi) round trip distance.

Due to the length of the journey, this spot is usually quiet. However, if based at the nearby backcountry campground, it is possible to visit at the almost-guaranteed-to-be-tranquil times of early morning or late evening.

The rocky shelves at the top of the falls grant vistas down Paradise Valley, and south over trees to Mt. Temple, Sentinel Pass with its rocky towers, Pinnacle Mountain, and Eiffel Peak. The precipitous east faces of Hungabee Mountain and Mt. Lefroy fill the gaze to the west.

Keep on the established trails described here to avoid causing trampling and erosion by using any of the faint paths that make a maze throughout the area.

**Giant Steps.**

# Sentinel Pass from Paradise Valley

**Distance:** 2.9 km (1.8 mi) — *Paradise Valley* trail to Sentinel Pass
**Day hike or backpack:** 1.5—2 hours one way
**Elevation gain:** 531 m (1742 ft)
**Maximum elevation:** 2611 m (8564 ft)
**Trailhead:** Km 8.7 on *Paradise Valley* trail (see p. 60). **N.B.** This trail and the *Paradise Valley* trail are subject to closure or voluntary restrictions (e.g., minimum party size) due to their location in grizzly bear habitat.

0.0 — Junction (elevation 2080 m). Turn left and cross long series of planks over creek.
0.1 — Pass unmarked junction with route to Wastach Pass (see page opposite).
0.6 — Keep right at junction (elevation 2110 m) with west end of *Lake Annette and Paradise Valley Highline* trail (see p. 62). Begin steep, rocky climb into north-facing basin that holds snow late.
2.9 — Sentinel Pass (2611 m).

Sentinel Pass can be reached by trail from Paradise Valley, but it is a longer and rougher approach than from the valley of Moraine Lake (see *Sentinel Pass from Larch Valley*, p. 74). If contemplating a trip connecting the two valleys, it is probably better to start at Moraine Lake since there is less elevation gain that way and the climbing is done earlier, followed by a long, gradual descent.

Because of its course through the sheltered basin north of Sentinel Pass, this trail often has snow late into summer and early in fall. This can make for treacherous footing, particularly in the steepest section near the summit of the pass. An ice axe or at least a hiking pole could well be necessary.

**Pinnacles above Sentinel Pass from Paradise Valley trail.**

## Captions for colour photographs

A bull moose with impressive antlers, met near the west end of Baker Lake. It was unnerving to have this powerful animal look intently at me for some time before moving into the trees, especially since it was autumn with the rut underway. The blooms of fireweed give pink highlights.

A midsummer view south from the knoll between Packer's Pass and Deception Pass. The entire length of Ptarmigan Lake fills the foreground; beyond are (l to r) Redoubt Lake, the soaring block of Redoubt Mountain, and Mt. Temple above Boulder Pass.

The bold turquoise of Moraine Lake stands out in this scene from the summit of Eiffel Peak. Above it are (l to r) Panorama Ridge with the Sawback Range beyond on the horizon, Mt. Babel (the Tower of Babel sits at the end of its north ridge), and Mt. Fay with the white expanse of the Fay Glacier spreading out below.

The fall needles of subalpine larch trees lend their orange hue to this panorama from the Big Beehive. The glaciated summits of Mts. Lefroy and Victoria stand out crisply in the clear September air.

Hidden Lake is revealed in this vista from Mt. Richardson. The lake's deep blue colour complements the white of snow lower on the south ridge and the green of meadows around the headwaters of Corral Creek.

The extensive meadows at the head of Paradise Valley stretch out below a vantage point on the moraine of the Horseshoe Glacier. In the distance between the walls hemming in the valley rise (l to r) Fossil Mountain, Redoubt Mountain, the summits of Mts. Douglas and St. Bride, Lipalian Mountain, and the twin peaks of "Little Temple."

Mottled brown plumage affords white-tailed ptarmigans excellent summer camouflage. I took this photograph in the meadows above the northwest shore of Merlin Lake.

Water cascades over a rock outcrop at the west end of Taylor Lake. The flow from the falls passes under a late-lying snowbank in this August composition.

The dark cones of subalpine fir stand up rather than hanging pendant like those of other conifers. This tree is beside the first of the switchbacks near the end of *The Plain of Six Glaciers* trail.

# Wastach Pass

**Distance:** 3.0 km (1.9 mi) — *Paradise Valley* trail to Wastach Pass
**Off-trail scramble:** 1.5—2 hours one way
**Elevation gain:** 461 m (1512 ft)
**Elevation loss:** 241 m (790 ft)
**Maximum elevation:** 2541 m (8334 ft)
**Trailhead:** Unmarked junction at km 0.1 on *Sentinel Pass from Paradise Valley* trail (see page opposite). **N.B.** This trail, the *Paradise Valley* trail, and the *Sentinel Pass from Paradise Valley* trail are subject to closure or voluntary restrictions (e.g., minimum party size) due to their location in grizzly bear habitat.

0.0 — Unmarked junction (elevation 2080 m). Head up to the south, aiming for the obvious draw between Eiffel Peak and the unnamed peak to its west. Snow remains below the pass on the north side well into summer.
2.4 — Wastach Pass (2541 m). Descend south.
3.0 — Join *Eiffel Lake* trail (2300 m) at km 3.2 (see p. 78).

Wastach Pass is an off-trail alternative to Sentinel Pass for travel between Paradise Valley and the Valley of the Ten Peaks. The name of this seldom-visited pass is the word in the language of the Stoney people for 'beautiful.' (Samuel Allen originally gave the name Wastach to the valley now known as Paradise.)

Route-finding to Wastach Pass from Paradise Valley is straightforward, although as with Sentinel Pass snow hangs on in the basin to the north and an ice axe or hiking pole could be called for. The rocky slopes just south of Wastach Pass are a good location to see the alpine specialty moss campion, a low cushion plant with a dazzling display of pink blossoms. (Take care not to trample this wildflower, which grows slowly and has a precarious hold in its challenging environment.)

The descent to Eiffel Lake is through a narrow gully (**Attention:** possible avalanche hazard) and over rocky slopes, with a semblance of trail in places.

**Scrambler John Blum and the author at Wastach Pass, with Paradise Valley to north.**

# Horseshoe Glacier

See photo p. 75, and sixth colour photo starting opposite p. 64.

**Distance:** Variable, depending on route taken
**Off-trail scramble:** Time variable
**Elevation gain:** 150 m (490 ft) maximum
**Maximum elevation:** 2240 m (7345 ft)
**Trailhead:** End of *Paradise Valley* trail at km 9.0 (see p. 60). **N.B.** The *Paradise Valley* trail that gives access to this area is subject to closure or voluntary restrictions (e.g., minimum party size) due to its location in grizzly bear habitat.

The terminal moraine of curving Horseshoe Glacier rises above larch-dotted Horseshoe Meadows at the head of Paradise Valley, where the backcountry campground is located. With experience, skill, and judgement, there are various possibilities for off-trail scrambling in the area.

One foray can be made by following up beside the stream that issues from the large, murky lake at the toe of the glacier. Once at the lake it is possible to complete its circumnavigation—if equipped with an ice axe at a minimum and, depending on conditions (e.g., snow cover), possibly glacier travel equipment (rope, harness, crampons, etc.), plus routefinding and rescue knowledge.

Circling the lake entails travelling up and down over steep moraine ridges and crossing over the heavily crevassed glacier. Note that the glacier ends in a sheer wall of ice up to 15 m (50 ft) high, with numerous waterfalls spilling over the lip to plunge straight into the west end of the lake. This area gives a view of a fascinating narrow tongue of ice that starts high up beneath some sharp pinnacles on the east ridge of Wenkchemna Peak and tumbles down toward the valley.

Another possible outing is to scramble over the debris-covered ice of the northern part of the Horseshoe Glacier to get a close look at a smaller, unnamed neighbouring glacier whose lateral moraines form symmetrical lobes encircling a small lake. This feature is visible from the *Sentinel Pass from Paradise Valley* trail, and it stands out especially well from the summits of Mt. Temple and Eiffel Peak.

To venture along the sharp crest of these moraines requires a good sense of balance, preferably assisted by an ice axe or a hiking pole. The grid reference of the centre of the small lake is 514895 on 1:50,000 scale topographic maps (NAD 83; see p. 19).

Although (as in the desert) the plants never grow near each other, the number of species that have colonized the Horseshoe Glacier is at least 20, astounding considering its initial appearance of a jumble of rocks and boulders.

Venturing over the Horseshoe Glacier takes one close beneath the imposing cliff bands on the southeast face of Mt. Lefroy and the east face of Hungabee Mountain. The latter's name means 'Chieftain' in the language of the Stoney people; the peak certainly is an impressive presence at the head of Paradise Valley.

**Moraines at base of Mitre Peak and cliff of Mt. Lefroy, from Horseshoe Glacier area.**

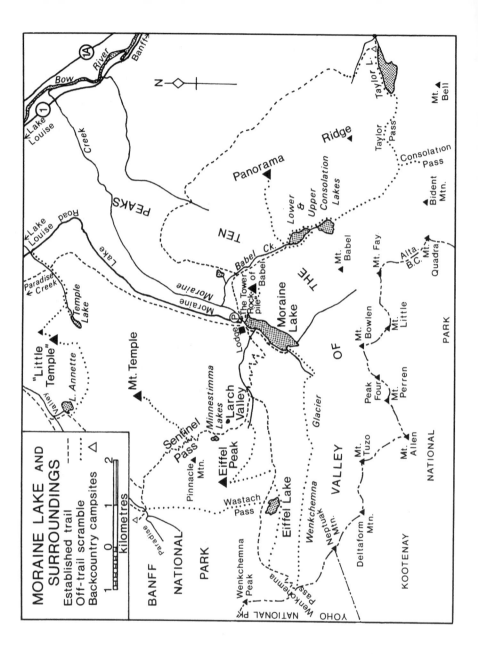

MORAINE LAKE AND
SURROUNDINGS

Established trail ------
Off-trail scramble ⋯⋯⋯
Backcountry campsites △

kilometres

# Moraine Lake and Surroundings

**Southern aspect of Mt. Temple from footbridge over Babel Creek just off *Lower Consolation Lake* trail at km 1.5.**

# The Rockpile

See photo p. 80.

**Distance:** 0.5 km (0.3 mi) — Moraine Lake parking area to top of the Rockpile
**Walk:** 15—20 minutes one way
**Elevation gain:** 15 m (50 ft)
**Maximum elevation:** 1900 m (6230 ft)
**Trailhead:** Southeast corner of Moraine Lake parking area, at the end of Moraine Lake Road which runs 11.5 km (7.1 mi) from its start 3.0 km (1.9 mi) along Lake Louise Drive (the route to Lake Louise itself) from Lake Louise Village. **N.B.** Moraine Lake Road is closed in winter (roughly October to May).

0.0 — Sign (elevation 1885 m). Go straight, away from parking area.
0.1 — Cross footbridge over Moraine Creek; go up short incline.
0.2 — Keep right at junction (1890 m) with *Lower Consolation Lake* trail (see p. 81). Climb rock-slab steps.
0.5 — 'Summit' of the Rockpile (1900 m).

The short interpretive trail up the Rockpile, the prominent heap of boulders at the northeast end of Moraine Lake, gives an excellent introduction to the famous Valley of the Ten Peaks. Viewpoints at and near the top give classic views of turquoise Moraine Lake and several of the Ten Peaks.

Walter Wilcox was spellbound by Moraine Lake, as we are today, but the name he gave it is misleading. He thought the lake was dammed by a terminal moraine pushed ahead at the toe of a glacier, but the modern theory is that the Rockpile originated in a massive rockslide. One piece of evidence is that the boulders are all of the same type, whereas a glacial moraine contains a mixture of rock types.

**Moraine Lake and several of the Ten Peaks from the Rockpile.**

# Moraine Lake Lakeshore

See third colour photo starting opposite p. 64.

**Distance:** 1.4 km (0.9 mi) — Parking area to southwest end of Moraine Lake
**Walk:** 20—30 minutes one way
**Elevation gain:** None
**Maximum elevation:** 1885 m (6185 ft)
**Trailhead:** South end of Moraine Lake parking area (see page opposite for access).

0.0 — South end of Moraine Lake parking area (elevation 1885 m). Continue straight on service road, passing in front of Moraine Lake Lodge.
0.2 — Keep left along north shore of Moraine Lake at junction with *Larch Valley* trail (see next page).
1.4 — Southwest end of Moraine Lake (1885 m).

As at Lake Louise, there is a trail along the north shore of Moraine Lake. This level trail allows a relaxing stroll along the lakeshore, with the possibility of seeing a mule deer along the way. The trail ends close to the meltwater stream running in from the Wenkchemna Glacier.

A highlight of this walk is the view—not possible from the north end of the lake near the parking area—of Mt. Fay, the first of the Ten Peaks, and its impressive Fay Glacier. The names honour Dr. Charles Fay, a mountaineer from Massachusetts who took part in many pioneering climbs in the vicinity.

The far end of Moraine Lake also gives a vantage point back down to the Rockpile at the opposite end, with the Tower of Babel (see p. 83) rising above it to the right. Canoeists are often seen on the lake: paddling is another enjoyable way to experience this famous body of water.

**Canoeists on Moraine Lake, with glaciated Mt. Fay on the skyline.**

# Larch Valley

**Distance:** 4.1 km (2.5 mi) — Moraine Lake to Larch Valley
**Day hike:** 1.5—2 hours one way
**Elevation gain:** 550 m (1805 ft)
**Maximum elevation:** 2435 m (7985 ft)
**Trailhead:** Km 0.2 on *Moraine Lake Lakeshore* trail (see previous page). **N.B.** This trail is subject to closure or voluntary restrictions (e.g., minimum party size) due to its location in grizzly bear habitat. [There is a plan to realign this trail away from bear territory.]

    0.0 — Keep right at junction (elevation 1885 m). Climb steadily on a series of switchbacks.
    2.4 — Keep right at junction (2260 m) with *Eiffel Lake* trail (see p. 78). Climb less steeply and travel through an open meadow flanked by subalpine larch trees.
    3.0 — Unmarked junction (2320 m) with off-trail scramble route up Eiffel Peak (see p. 77).
    3.6 — Treelimit (2385 m).
    4.1 — Largest of the Minnestimma Lakes (2435 m).

    The hike to Larch Valley ranks as one of the more popular outings in Banff National Park, especially in autumn when the trees after which it is named display a radiant golden glow. (This trail can be very crowded in the fall, especially on weekends—other good areas for subalpine larches are the Saddleback (p. 48), the meadows above Taylor Lake (pages 124 and 84), and the slopes around Boulder Pass (p. 98).)
    The first stands of larch soon appear after keeping right at km 2.4, followed by a fair-sized meadow. Mt. Temple (see p. 75) rises loftily to the north, while ahead stand Pinnacle Mountain and Eiffel Peak (see p. 77).

**Hikers in meadow on *Larch Valley* trail; Eiffel Peak in distance.**

**Deltaform Mountain and ridge of Eiffel Peak reflected in largest Minnestimma Lake.**

After the meadow, the trail leads up steadily to reach the last trees at about km 3.6. Five hundred metres farther on lies the largest of the Minnestimma Lakes sprinkled in the bowl between Mt. Temple and Pinnacle Mountain. The name of these tarns, which has the evocative translation 'sleeping water,' was given by explorer/mountaineer Samuel Allen (who had the assistance of William Twin of the Stoney people in choosing the many names from their language that he bestowed on features).

Of Allen's original Stoney-numeral names for the summits on the south side of the Valley of the Ten Peaks, only those for Neptuak (nine) and Wenkchemna (ten) survive. The others have had newer names conferred upon them, often of people connected with more recent history...of which perhaps the most appropriate is Mt. Allen, formerly Shappee (six).

# Sentinel Pass from Larch Valley

**Distance:** 1.7 km (1.1 mi) — End of *Larch Valley* trail to Sentinel Pass
**Extension to day hike or backpack:** 45 minutes one way
**Elevation gain:** 176 m (577 ft)
**Maximum elevation:** 2611 m (8564 ft)
**Trailhead:** End of *Larch Valley* trail at km 4.1 (see two previous pages). **N.B.** The *Larch Valley* trail and this trail are subject to closure or voluntary restrictions (e.g., minimum party size) due to their location in grizzly bear habitat.

0.0 — South shore of largest Minnestimma Lake (elevation 2435 m). Turn right away from lake and head up steady switchbacks.
1.7 — Sentinel Pass (2611 m).

Continuing from the end of the *Larch Valley* trail, this steep climb leads to the narrow gap of Sentinel Pass. This trail is the highest maintained one in Banff National Park. The well-defined zigzags are readily seen from below, giving a clear picture of what's ahead when tackling this trail. The total elevation gain from Moraine Lake is 726 m (almost 2400 ft).

The pass grants superb vistas from its height of over 2600 m, including north over Paradise Valley. In that direction but not all the way down to the valley rises the Grand Sentinel, the freestanding pillar that is the tallest of those on Pinnacle Mountain that give the pass its name.

The *Sentinel Pass from Paradise Valley* trail (see p. 64) leads onward, though the way is rougher and snow often hangs in on the north-facing slopes below the pass (**N.B.**, an ice axe or hiking pole may be required). A full-day trip can be made by taking that trail and continuing to the Moraine Lake Road via Lake Annette (see pages 62 and 60). Taking into account the significant climb and the total distance from Moraine Lake for this excursion of 17.6 km (10.9 mi), it's a good idea to arrange transportation at the Paradise Valley trailhead once finished.

**Pinnacles north of Sentinel Pass.**

# Mt. Temple

See photos p. 8, p. 16, p. 26, p. 50, p. 69, p. 76, p. 85, and p. 123.

**Distance:** 2.0 km (1.2 mi) — Sentinel Pass to summit of Mt. Temple
**Off-trail scramble:** 2—3 hours one way
**Elevation gain:** 932 m (3057 ft)
**Maximum elevation:** 3543 m (11,621 ft)
**Trailhead:** Sentinel Pass (see page opposite). **N.B.** The *Larch Valley* and *Sentinel Pass* trails that give access to Mt. Temple are subject to closure or voluntary restrictions (e.g., minimum party size) due to their location in grizzly bear habitat.

0.0 — Sentinel Pass (elevation 2611 m). Turn east at summit of pass (right as coming from Moraine Lake) and head up scree slope toward the base of a pinnacle known as The Tooth. Traverse right beneath a high buttress; later gain the southwest ridge via suitable gullies—don't continue on a traverse out onto the face, despite possible cairns. Take quite well-defined switchbacks up to the false summit at km 1.7, then ascend gentler slope. (**N.B.** Beware cornices on this final section.)

2.0 — Summit of Mt. Temple (3543 m).

The attempt to ascend Mt. Temple from Sentinel Pass is an ambitious undertaking requiring thorough preparation and experience in navigation, despite following what is known in climbing circles as the 'Tourist Route:' a nickname given in comparison with the highly technical north-face climb.

Keep in mind that getting to the summit of Mt. Temple involves gaining as much again, and then some, as to Sentinel Pass. Plus the route is at a much steeper angle. Come prepared with proper gear and the proper respect for the tenth-highest peak in the Canadian Rockies and the highest point in the Lake Louise area. **N.B.** It is advisable to have an ice axe or hiking pole. (cont. next page)

**Vista including Horseshoe Glacier and Hungabee Mountain (l) from Mt. Temple's top.**

**Scramblers descending from the summit of Mt. Temple.**

(Cont. from previous page)

Attaining the summit of Mt. Temple entails an ascent of over 1650 m (more than a vertical mile) from Moraine Lake. A plethora of cairns can cause confusion on the ascent; keep in mind that people have perished on this mountain.

The recompense of gaining the top is the sight (if conditions allow) of a veritable sea of peaks...this can be a great place to get out the map and binoculars so as to identify many landmarks.

Mt. Temple is the third highest peak in Banff National Park, after Mt. Assiniboine (3618 m) and Mt. Forbes (3612 m). Its name commemorates Sir Richard Temple, who visited the Lake Louise area during an 1884 field trip of the British Association for the Advancement of Science, of which he was president. Rather more sublime, the mountain's name also suggests a place worthy—with its stupendous cliffs and shimmering glacial cap—of whatever form of worship one might practise.

While at the top of Mt. Temple, ravens might be spotted: despite such a rarefied height, these hardy birds are at home. They might soar past, issuing their unexpectedly varied calls, or perhaps alight close by out of curiosity. As Peter Matthiessen wrote in his classic **The Snow Leopard**, ravens (though often taken as ominous) are harbingers of life, persistently tenacious even in high, cold regions.

# Eiffel Peak

See photos p. 72, p. 73, and third colour photo starting opposite p. 64.

**Distance:** 2.2 km (1.4 mi) — *Larch Valley* trail to summit of Eiffel Peak
**Off-trail scramble:** 1.5—2 hours one way
**Elevation gain:** 764 m (2506 ft)
**Maximum elevation:** 3084 m (10,116 ft)
**Trailhead:** Km 3.0 on *Larch Valley* trail (see p. 72). **N.B.** The *Larch Valley* trail and this route are subject to closure or voluntary restrictions (e.g., minimum party size) due to their location in grizzly bear habitat.

0.0 — Unmarked junction (elevation 2320 m) on *Larch Valley* trail. Descend slightly to cross a creek, then work up to treed lower section of southeast ridge of Eiffel Peak. Proceed up talus and scree, choosing a gully to get through the rock band, then scrambling up debris-covered slabs to the summit.

2.2 — Summit of Eiffel Peak (3084 m).

Eiffel Peak gives the easiest ascent of a peak over 3000 m (about 10,000 ft) in the Lake Louise area. It is nevertheless a strenuous outing; to climb Eiffel Peak requires experience in scrambling over talus (boulders) and scree (smaller rocks), both of which are liable to shift suddenly. This trip also calls for routefinding skills.

It is only once at the top on this route that it becomes possible to see the impressive rock tower on the north side of the peak. The mountain got its name because of the tower's fancied resemblance to the Eiffel Tower.

**The rock tower adjacent to Eiffel Peak, seen from the summit.**

# Eiffel Lake

**Distance:** 3.2 km (2.0 mi) — *Larch Valley* trail to above Eiffel Lake
**Extension to day hike:** 45 minutes—1 hour one way
**Elevation gain:** 40 m (130 ft)
**Maximum elevation:** 2300 m (7545 ft)
**Trailhead:** Km 2.4 on *Larch Valley* trail (see p. 72). **N.B.** The *Larch Valley* trail and this trail are subject to closure or voluntary restrictions (e.g., minimum party size) due to their location in grizzly bear habitat.

0.0 — Sign at junction (elevation 2260 m). Keep left along mostly level trail passing along southern base of Eiffel Peak.
3.2 — Unmarked point (2300 m) directly above north shore of Eiffel Lake.

Although less likely to receive visits than nearby Larch Valley (especially in autumn), Eiffel Lake is an interesting destination in its own right, one that gives a feeling for the wilderness character of the head of the Valley of the Ten Peaks.

An attractive feature of this jaunt is that after having climbed almost 400 m to its start, this trail gives a breather. Its 3.2 km stay virtually level, following close to a contour along the southern slopes of Eiffel Peak. There is also the reward of open stretches with views from high up of Moraine Lake, the Wenkchemna Glacier, and all of the Ten Peaks.

The trail does not go to Eiffel Lake itself, staying to the north about fifty metres above its deep, clear, blue-green waters. For a closer appreciation, it is possible to scramble down to the lake's edge. A circumnavigation of Eiffel Lake allows views from its south side of Eiffel Peak, after which the lake is named. And going a little west of the lake gives a glimpse of the rock tower adjacent to Eiffel Peak, after which the mountain in turn got its name (see previous page).

An off-trail scramble north from the end of this trail leads to Wastach Pass, on the other side of which lies Paradise Valley (see p. 65).

**Eiffel Lake from the east, with Wenkchemna Pass and Peak and Hungabee Mountain.**

# Wenkchemna Pass

See photo on page opposite.

**Distance:** 4.1 km (2.5 mi) — End of *Eiffel Lake* trail to Wenkchemna Pass
**Extension to day hike:** 1.5 hours one way
**Elevation gain:** 300 m (985 ft)
**Maximum elevation:** 2600 m (8530 ft)
**Trailhead:** End of *Eiffel Lake* trail (see page opposite). **N.B.** The *Larch Valley* and *Eiffel Lake* trails that give access to Wenkchemna Pass are subject to closure or voluntary restrictions (e.g., minimum party size) due to their location in grizzly bear habitat.


0.0 — Unmarked point (elevation 2300 m) directly above north shore of Eiffel Lake. Continue straight, climbing gradually at first, then more steeply up switchbacks (often snow-covered).
4.1 — Wenkchemna Pass (2600 m).

Wenkchemna Pass is the major saddle in the Ten Peaks between Neptuak (Stoney for 'nine') Mountain and Wenkchemna ('ten') Peak: these are the only ones of the 10 summits that still hold the names given to them by Samuel Allen in the 1890s.

A blast of cold air will likely be the greeting that Wenkchemna Pass offers, standing as it does on the continental divide and thus also sitting on the Alberta/British Columbia boundary. To the west is Yoho National Park, with Curtis Peak above the valley below that holds the pinnacle known as Eagle Eyrie. A short distance to the south, in Kootenay National Park (the boundaries of the three parks meet on top of Neptuak Mountain), is Prospector Valley, as the headwaters of Tokumm Creek are known. [Prospector Valley is prime grizzly bear habitat.]

Late-lying snow patches, still present in mid-September in most years, can make it hard to pick out the way while going up to Wenkchemna Pass. However, once ready to leave they can also have a positive effect (if properly prepared with an ice axe) by providing the opportunity for a speedy initial descent via a glissade.

**East from Wenkchemna Pass over moraines of the Wenkchemna Glacier to Mt. Babel.**

# Wenkchemna Glacier

See photo p. 79.

**Distance:** 7.0 km 4.3 mi) — Wenkchemna Pass to Moraine Lake
**Off-trail scramble:** 2—3 hours one way
**Elevation loss:** 715 m (2345 ft)
**Maximum elevation:** 2600 m (8530 ft)
**Trailhead:** Wenkchemna Pass (see previous page). **N.B.** The *Larch Valley* and *Eiffel Lake* trails that give access to Wenkchemna Pass, and the area traversed on this off-trail route, are subject to closure or voluntary restrictions (e.g., minimum party size) due to their location in grizzly bear habitat.

0.0 — Wenkchemna Pass (elevation 2600 m). Head over the moraines of the Wenkchemna Glacier, staying north of the crevassed section of the glacier. **N.B.** Beware of unstable areas of moraine, of icy sections covered with a thin veneer of moraine, and of the presence of water-filled sinkholes with steep icy sides.
7.0 — South end (1885 m) of *Moraine Lake Lakeshore* trail (see p. 71).

Descending the moraines of the Wenkchemna Glacier is an option for dedicated cross-country travellers. This 'rock-hopper's special' involves lots of up-and-down navigation in jumbled terrain that makes it easy to understand why this was originally called 'Desolation Valley.'

The moraines can be left after about 4.0 km, moving off to the north to follow the generally open margin beside the wall of stones and boulders (about 10 m high here). About 500 m later, a faint path leads to the origin of Moraine Creek, gushing out from the terminal moraine.

Descending beside the creek on its south side allows one glimpse of Moraine Lake and the Rockpile (see p. 70) at its east end. Cross the creek on primitive footbridges used by mountaineers heading for ascents of the Ten Peaks, and pick up the well-used *Moraine Lake Lakeshore* trail. This leads back to the parking area to complete an unusual variation.

**East down Moraine Creek to Moraine Lake and the Rockpile.**

# Lower Consolation Lake

See photos p. 29, p. 69, p. 82, and p. 85.

**Distance:** 2.8 km (1.7 mi) — *The Rockpile* trail to Lower Consolation Lake
**Day hike:** 1 hour one way
**Elevation gain:** 55 m (180 ft)
**Maximum elevation:** 1945 m (6380 ft)
**Trailhead:** Km 0.2 on *The Rockpile* trail (see p. 70).

0.0 — Junction on *The Rockpile* trail (elevation 1890 m). Keep straight.
0.3 — Junction (1895 m), possibly unmarked, with off-trail route up the Tower of Babel (see p. 83).
1.5 — Keep straight at junction (1930 m) with *Taylor Lake from Valley of the Ten Peaks* unmaintained trail (see p. 84).
2.2 — Arrive at open, boggy meadow adjacent to Babel Creek.
2.8 — Babel Creek near north end of Lower Consolation Lake (1945 m).

Consolation Valley, southeast of Moraine Lake, received its name because of its beauty in comparison with the upper reaches of the Valley of the Ten Peaks, originally called 'Desolation Valley.' Today the consolation to be found in this valley comes in the form of respite from busier parts of the Lake Louise area.

The trail to Lower Consolation Lake passes through subalpine forest with a high density of porcupines. The author has even come across a porcupine in an unlikely location among the rocks near the lake (see photo below).

(cont. next page)

**Porcupine photographed among rocks near Lower Consolation Lake.**

(Cont. from previous page)

Evidence of the often misunderstood and sometimes maligned porcupine is visible (even if the animals themselves are not) in the shape of quills on the ground. There is still a widespread belief that porcupines can 'shoot' their spiny armour. This is not so. Before the barbed quills can hold, they must penetrate the skin of an attacker—which the porcupine accomplishes by lashing about with its tail.

Subalpine fir trees (see eighth page of colour photos starting opposite p. 64) can be seen that have had the smooth outer layer of bark gnawed off by porcupines. The animals do this to reach the cambium, the thin inner layer before the hard heartwood. The cambium is high in natural sugars and plant proteins. Although porcupines occasionally girdle a tree, resulting in its death, this is not detrimental in an ecological sense. The nutrients are recycled into the soil and can provide the basis for new trees to get established, thus supplying food for future generations of porcupines.

The open meadow reached at km 2.2 on the *Lower Consolation Lake* trail gives views of Panorama Ridge (see p. 87) to the east. To the south lies Consolation Pass (see p. 86) at the head of the valley. The glacier-draped cliffs of Mt. Quadra (with four peaks) and Bident Mountain (two peaks) add to a spectacular setting.

The established trail ends at Babel Creek; to reach the shore of the lake calls for scrambling over large, angular boulders. There are subalpine larch trees near the finish, as well as cushions of moss campion with pink flowers when in bloom. Hoary marmots are usually in evidence in the environs.

It is possible to continue to Upper Consolation Lake (see p. 85).

**View from the Tower of Babel of Lower Consolation Lake (foreground) as well as the upper lake and (l to r) Panorama Ridge, Taylor Pass, Mt. Bell, and Consolation Pass.**

# The Tower of Babel

See photos on page opposite, on p. 85, and third colour photo starting opposite p. 64.

**Distance:** 1.1 km (0.7 mi) — *Lower Consolation Lake* trail to summit of the Tower of Babel
**Off-trail scramble:** 1—1.5 hour(s) one way
**Elevation gain:** 405 m (1330 ft)
**Maximum elevation:** 2300 m (7545 ft)
**Trailhead:** Km 0.3 on *Lower Consolation Lake* trail (see p. 81).

0.0 — Point (elevation 1895 m) on *Lower Consolation Lake* trail. Turn south off trail [the route may be marked by a cairn, e.g., on a large boulder 15 m in] and head over scree [possible faint path] to base of obvious gully to the west (right) of the Tower of Babel. **N.B.** The ascent of this gully leaves one seriously exposed to rockfall (there have been injuries). Wear a helmet, try to go up early in the day when it is less likely a party above will dislodge something, and take care not to kick stones down either on the ascent or on the descent. The route is not feasible for non-alpinists if it has snow in it.

0.8 — Top of gully. Turn hard left.

1.1 — Summit of the Tower of Babel (2300 m).

The Tower of Babel is the imposing isolated quartzite feature at the end of the long north ridge of Mt. Babel. Its sheer (in places overhanging) cliffs were first scaled by rockclimbers in 1957.

However, it is not necessary to use technical equipment to reach the top of the tower (although a helmet is highly recommended). The summit is accessible via a scramble up the steep, narrow gully on its west side. Keep in mind that this route involves lots of scree-churning, and—as stated above—rockfall hazard. A line on either side of the gully is much preferable to going up the centre.

Once up the gully, the grade eases to the large flat expanse at the summit. This plateau gives good views to the southeast over Consolation Valley. [Another approach to the Tower of Babel is from Lower Consolation Lake: although the rockfall hazard is reduced, this involves tiring, difficult bushwhacking through subalpine fir trees in avalanche paths and is not recommended.]

Climbing down a small rockband from the top of the Tower of Babel allows views (with care due to the cliff below) almost straight down onto the Rockpile, which appears flat from this vantage point, and onto the north end of Moraine Lake.

# Taylor Lake from Valley of the Ten Peaks

**Distance:** 11.5 km (7.1 mi) — *Lower Consolation Lake* trail to Taylor Lake
**Unmaintained trail:** 3.5—4 hours one way
**Elevation gain:** 355 m (1165 ft)
**Elevation loss:** 220 m (720 ft)
**Maximum elevation:** 2285 m (7495 ft)
**Trailhead:** Km 1.5 on *Lower Consolation Lake* trail (see p. 81).

0.0 — Junction (elevation 1930 m). Turn east off the *Lower Consolation Lake* trail and descend slightly to cross Babel Creek via a footbridge in 50 m.

0.4 — Pass to south of a small, marshy lake.

1.3 — Sharp turn downhill to left (do not continue straight). Trail then runs level for several hundred metres before beginning to climb.

5.0 — High point (2285 m). Trail is very faint across meadows beyond; stay on a generally level course.

9.7 — Pass by remains of old cabins; there is also evidence of former mines in the area. The trail disappears in a large meadow 200 m beyond; head southeast.

11.0 — Pick up the trail again on the south side of the main creek.

11.5 — Taylor Lake (2065 m) and backcountry campground (see p. 124 for the usual approach from the Trans-Canada Highway).

Despite all sorts of markings, such as blazes (axe markings) on trees, pieces of survey tape tied in conspicuous locations, occasional wooden survey stakes with red paint on top, small rock cairns, and fallen logs that have been cut in the course of trail clearing, this currently unmaintained trail can be difficult to follow.

Confusion can arise when crossing a series of meadows and avalanche paths. In general, keep at the same elevation or slightly higher while searching for the trail at the opposite end of an open area in which it has disappeared. (It's harder to find the way if facing into the sun.)

A compensation for the navigational challenges of this trail is the travel through the zone of subalpine larch, especially enjoyable in fall. And traces of human history are present in the shape of old mine workings and long-abandoned cabins.

The end is nigh once a large, larch-fringed meadow comes into sight. Follow southeast down its watercourses to rejoin the well-defined trail on the south side of the main creek. This leads to Taylor Lake and its backcountry campground. The options here include descending the *Taylor Lake from Trans-Canada Highway* trail (see p. 124) or continuing southeast beneath the ridge of Mt. Bell to visit O'Brien Lake or connect with the *Boom Lake* trail and exit to Highway 93 South (see the author's **Backcountry Banff** guidebook, also published by Luminous Compositions).

# Upper Consolation Lake

See photo p. 82.

**Distance:** 1.4 km (0.9 mi) — End of *Lower Consolation Lake* trail to Upper Consolation Lake
**Unmaintained trail and off-trail scramble:** 30 minutes one way
**Elevation gain:** 15 m (50 ft)
**Maximum elevation:** 1960 m (6430 ft)
**Trailhead:** End of *Lower Consolation Lake* trail (see p. 81).

0.0 — End of *Lower Consolation Lake* trail (elevation 1945 m). Ford Babel Creek to east side, turn south (right) through marshy area, and pick up narrow path along the east shore of Lower Consolation Lake.
1.1 — South end of Lower Consolation Lake. Continue south, climbing slightly over rockslide.
1.4 — North end of Upper Consolation Lake (1960 m).

A huge rockslide divides what was once a single body of water into two lakes, which a British barrister on a guided walk led by the author during his Parks Canada career suggested could be called 'Consolation' and 'More Consolation.' Even if his proposal has not been adopted, it is indeed rewarding to venture to the upper lake, which is even quieter and more peaceful than the easily accessible lower lake.

Although it is possible to 'rock-hop' around the lower lake along the west side, there is rockfall hazard from the precipitous east face of Mt. Babel, and it is easier to take the faint path along the east side. First, though, Babel Creek must be forded, and the going once across can be boggy for a while. Head away from the bank of the creek to pick up a narrow path at the edge of the trees. Even here the route can be wet and muddy.

Marmots may be seen, including in the rocky avalanche path crossed en route to the upper lake. (Even on a summer day, do look up to make sure that no snow from high above will come roaring down having been loosened by the warmth.)

**Mt. Temple and the Tower of Babel from the south end of Lower Consolation Lake, en route to Upper Consolation Lake.**

# Consolation Pass

See photo p. 82.

**Distance:** 3.5 km (2.2 mi) — Upper Consolation Lake to Consolation Pass
**Off-trail scramble:** 2—2.5 hours one way
**Elevation gain:** 515 m (1690 ft)
**Maximum elevation:** 2475 m (8120 ft)
**Trailhead:** North end of Upper Consolation Lake (see previous page).

0.0 — North end of Upper Consolation Lake (elevation 1960 m). Proceed along the east shore of Upper Consolation Lake to its south end. Climb onto the well-defined east lateral moraine and follow along its wide crest, then turn southeast up the cirque.

3.0 — Approximate point (about 2265 m) at which the route over Taylor Pass (see p. 125) joins this route. The final 500 m to Consolation Pass involves an elevation gain of over 200 m up a slope that remains snow-covered late into summer. **N.B.** Ice axe required at a minimum; avalanche hazard.

3.5 — Consolation Pass (2475 m).

The trip to Consolation Pass is an adventurous option for experienced off-trail travellers. Hiking along the east lateral moraine is almost like being on a maintained trail, and its height above the glacier gives an unusual perspective over an expanse of ice-cored moraine. Interspersed about the glacier are occasional steep-sided, water-filled kettle holes, formed when a remnant ice block melts and the moraine collapses into the hole.

From the head of the cirque it is a quasi-technical ascent to gain the pass: an ice axe will come into play on the steep snow, and the angle is such that some might prefer being roped up with at least one partner.

An option from the head of the cirque below Consolation Pass is to head cross-country to the easier (but still no picnic) saddle between Panorama Ridge and Mt. Bell: see the *Taylor Pass* description (p. 125).

**Looking south from Consolation Pass on a November visit.**

# Panorama Ridge

See photo p. 82 and third colour photo starting opposite p. 64.

**Distance:** 2.4 km (1.5 mi) — *Lower Consolation Lake* trail to high point at the north end of Panorama Ridge
**Off-trail scramble:** 2—2.5 hours one way
**Elevation gain:** 875 m (2870 ft)
**Maximum elevation:** 2820 m (9250 ft)
**Trailhead:** End of *Lower Consolation Lake* trail (see p. 81).

0.0 — End of *Lower Consolation Lake* trail (elevation 1945 m). Ford Babel Creek, then head easterly to zigzag up prominent avalanche gully. [**N.B.** Beware of any late-lying snow that, loosened by warm temperatures, could come thundering down.] Cut right before the cliffs at the gully's apex, and continue to the summit ridge. Turn south (right) to small cairn.

2.4 — High point at north end of Panorama Ridge (2820 m).

The name Panorama Ridge is intriguing enough to warrant a visit to experience the views firsthand. Although there is access to Panorama Ridge via the northeast spur from the *Taylor Lake from Valley of the Ten Peaks* unmaintained trail (see the author's book **Ridgewalks in the Canadian Rockies,** Luminous Compositions), the route described here is more direct.

The top of the north end of the ridge does indeed present a panorama. The landmarks visible include the surrounding peaks to the west: (l to r) Bident Mountain, Mt. Quadra, Mt. Fay, Mt. Babel, and Mt. Temple. There are also views down to the Consolation Lakes and far up the valley of Baker Creek (now mostly closed to foot travel; see p. 117).

The south end of Panorama Ridge is the higher but its towers of broken rock are not conducive to ropeless scrambling.

**Southeast from Panorama Ridge to the Bow Valley and surrounding peaks.**

# Paradise Creek from Moraine Lake

**Distance:** 8.4 km (5.2 mi) — Moraine Lake to *Paradise Valley* trail
**Day hike:** 2 hours one way
**Elevation gain:** 145 m (475 ft)
**Elevation loss:** 230 m (755 ft)
**Maximum elevation:** 2025 m (6640 ft)
**Trailhead:** Southwest corner of Moraine Lake parking area (see p. 70 for access).
**N.B.** This trail is subject to closure or voluntary restrictions (e.g., minimum party size) due to its location in grizzly bear habitat. Also note that this trail, if open, is designated for mountain biking.

0.0 — Sign (elevation 1885 m). Follow gravel path over small bridge and up a series of steps to join the original trail.
4.7 — High point on trail (2025 m).
5.2 — Cross creek (1985 m) feeding from Temple Lake (see page opposite).
8.3 — Footbridge (1795 m) over Paradise Creek.
8.4 — *Paradise Valley* trail (1800 m) at km 1.1 (see p. 60).

The initial section of this trail runs not far above Moraine Lake Road: the traffic below can be heard and sometimes seen. However, these are minor drawbacks when taking into account the open vistas obtained along the sunny south-facing slope. Among the views are the south face of Mt. Temple looming above. [**N.B.** Beware the slide hazard in the avalanche slopes that must be crossed.]

The dry conditions on the first part of this trail are manifest in vegetation such as locoweed, juniper, and mountain ash. The trail climbs 140 m as it rounds the east ridge of Mt. Temple, then descends steadily through closed coniferous forest where a spruce grouse might be spotted.

**Temple Lake.**

# Temple Lake and 'Little Temple'

See photo on page opposite, and sixth colour photo starting opposite p. 64.

**Distance:** 2.7 km (1.7 mi) — *Paradise Creek from Moraine Lake* trail to summit of 'Little Temple'
**Extension to day hike and off-trail scramble:** 30—40 minutes one way to Temple Lake; an additional 1—1.5 hour(s) one way to summit of 'Little Temple'
**Elevation gain:** 200 m (655 ft) to Temple Lake; an additional 475 m (1560 ft) to summit of 'Little Temple'
**Maximum elevation:** 2660 m (8725 ft)
**Trailhead:** Km 5.2 on *Paradise Creek from Moraine Lake* trail (see page opposite).

0.0 —Unmarked junction (elevation 1985 m) on south side of creek issuing from Temple Lake.. Head up rough, unmaintained path (lots of windfall).

0.7 — Path crosses to north side of creek.

1.4 — Temple Lake (2185 m). To climb 'Little Temple,' head up the mostly open slope north of the east end of the lake, heading for the east peak.

2.3 — East peak (2645 m) of 'Little Temple.' Traverse ridge to the southwest to reach the west peak.

2.7 — West peak and true summit (2660 m) of 'Little Temple.'

Temple Lake is a small gem lying in a tightly enclosed cirque beneath the east face of Mt. Temple. The rough path to it is most often used by anglers, although it appears that most of the fish in the lake are rather small. This is a typical alpine tarn: ice from the surrounding snowbanks can be found floating in it even in August. A circumnavigation of the lake could be an enjoyable finale to a visit this far.

The optional scramble up 'Little Temple' (unofficial name of this lesser peak close to Mt. Temple) leads to an impressive vantage point. The views might have to be shared with some mountain goats but that's not a problem eh?.

It is possible to descend south from the west peak to the 2425 m col [impassable on its east side] between 'Little Temple' and Mt. Temple. From here, descent can be continued west down an obvious gully (not glaciated, despite the possible indication on some maps) to Lake Annette. The distance to the lake from the summit is 2.7 km (1.7 mi). From Lake Annette, established trails lead to Moraine Lake Road (see pages 62 and 60).

Speaking of Moraine Lake Road, an optional connector to the start of this trail begins from a small parking area on the east side of the road 6.0 km (3.7 mi) from where it branches off Lake Louise Drive. This more direct approach rises beside the creek, gaining approximately 100 m (330 ft) over its 600 m length.

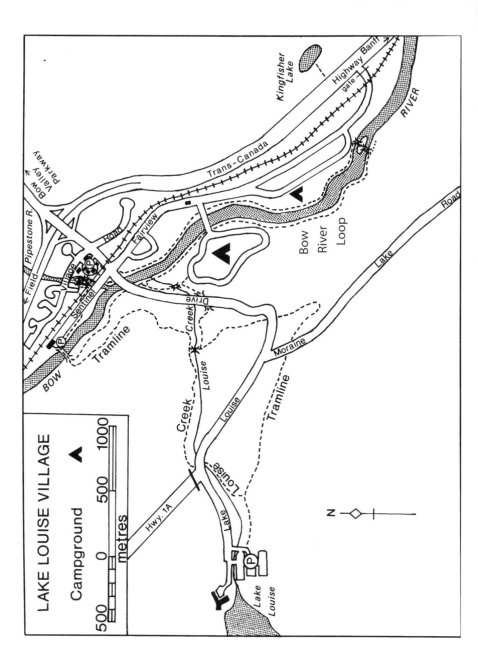

LAKE LOUISE VILLAGE

Campground ▲

metres

500   0   500   1000

# Around Lake Louise Village

**Black-capped chickadee.**

# Bow River Loop

See photo on page opposite.

**Distance:** 7.1 km (4.4 mi) — Loop that can begin at any of several points
**Walk:** 1.5—2 hours for entire loop
**Elevation gain:** Negligible
**Maximum elevation:** 1535 m (5035 ft)
**Trailhead:** Various options, including the parking areas at the end of Sentinel Road, the Lake Louise Information Centre/Samson Mall parking area, and the Lake Louise frontcountry campgrounds. The description below starts at the first option, where it is usually easier to find parking: at the second four-way stop off the Trans-Canada Highway, turn north (right) onto Sentinel Road and drive 0.9 km (0.6 mi) to its end. Park to the west. **N.B.** This trail is open to mountain biking.

0.0 — Cross Bow River on footbridge (elevation 1535 m) and turn left along the river; *Tramline* trail goes to the right (see page opposite).

0.8 — Cross Lake Louise Drive and continue straight down embankment; *Louise Creek* trail goes off to the right on the far side of the road (see p. 94). Pass through gate in bear-proof fencing.

1.7 — Cross access road to tenting section of Lake Louise campground and continue straight. Pass by trailer court (scheduled to be removed) in 300 m.

3.5 — Turn left to cross Bow River on two footbridges connecting an island to the banks. Turn left again to travel along the east bank.

5.3 — Cross access road leading over bridge to tenting section of Lake Louise campground and continue straight.

6.3 — Cross Lake Louise Drive and keep straight. The Lake Louise Information Centre and Samson Mall are 250 m away to the right via the trail that passes under the railway overpass.

6.4 — Cross Pipestone River on road bridge and continue along the road. (A connector to the Lake Louise Information Centre and Samson Mall goes right to pass under the low railway bridge [flooding hazard] toward the Post Hotel, then takes footbridges over the Pipestone River.)

6.6 — Veer left off Sentinel Road to travel beside the east bank of the Bow River.

7.1 — Return to the trailhead (1535 m).

This walk beside the Bow River, formerly known as the *Riverside* trail, makes for a relaxing amble close to Lake Louise Village. Although the trail passes near developed areas, the river is a constant reminder of natural processes. Its milky colour is due to glacial meltwater, and its volume varies with the season, being highest during spring runoff. A bonus in early summer might be sighting harlequin ducks bobbing on the wild current or resting on small islands. The males have a distinctive plumage of chestnut, white, black, and grey, while the mostly beige females sport a prominent white patch on the side of the head.

This trail features a rich variety of colourful wildflowers. Look for bird's-eye primrose, heart-leaved arnica, rock jasmine, shooting star, Western Canada violet, and bracted honeysuckle. [The author's best-selling **Central Rockies Wildflowers** (Luminous Compositions) is a compact guide to these species and most others in the area.]

# Tramline

**Distance:** 4.5 km (2.8 mi) — Bow River to Lake Louise
**Day hike:** 1—1.5 hour(s) one way
**Elevation gain:** 195 m (640 ft)
**Maximum elevation:** 1730 m (5675 ft)
**Trailhead:** Same as for *Bow River Loop* trail (see page opposite). **N.B.** This trail is open to mountain biking.

0.0 — Cross Bow River on footbridge (elevation 1535 m) and turn right, then quickly veer left and begin climbing; to the left along the river is the *Bow River Loop* trail (see page opposite).

0.7 — Open area.

1.5 — Keep straight at junction and cross footbridge shared in common with the *Louise Creek* trail (which continues across a smaller footbridge up to the right and comes in from down on the left after the footbridge; see next page).

2.2 — Cross Lake Louise Drive (Caution: traffic). The trail later swings through a wide turn.

2.9 — Cross Moraine Lake Road (Caution: traffic).

4.1 — Keep straight at junction (1725 m) with end of the *Louise Creek* trail.

4.5 — Eastern end of lower Lake Louise parking area (1730 m).

This trail follows the route used by trams between 1912 and 1930 to take guests from the train station in the valley up to the Chateau Lake Louise. The tracks are gone but the constant grade makes for good hiking.

The trail mostly passes through forest but the open area at km 0.7 gives a fine vantage southeast over the Bow Valley.

**Male harlequin duck on the Bow River.**

# Louise Creek

**Distance:** 2.3 km (1.4 mi) — Bow River to *Tramline* trail just below Lake Louise
**Day hike:** 1—1.25 hour(s) one way
**Elevation gain:** 190 m (625 ft)
**Maximum elevation:** 1725 m (5660 ft)
**Trailhead:** Km 0.8 on *Bow River Loop* trail (see p. 92). There is no parking at this trailhead; the options include parking at the north end of Sentinel Drive (as described on p. 92) and hiking 800 m along the *Bow River Loop* trail, parking in the Information Centre/Samson Mall parking area and walking about 400 m to the trailhead, or if staying at the campground using the connector that links with this trail near km 0.4.

  0.0 — Junction (elevation 1535 m) at bottom of embankment below Lake Louise Drive on its south side. Keep right; *Bow River Loop* trail goes left.

  0.3 — Cross footbridge over Louise Creek and turn right.

  0.4 — Cross another footbridge; connector trail shortly beyond leads left to the campground. Climb to pass through culvert under Lake Louise Drive, then contour back toward Louise Creek.

  1.0 — Turn right at junction with *Tramline* trail (see previous page) and cross footbridge that this trail has in common with it to reach km 1.5 junction on *Tramline* trail. Turn left over smaller footbridge and head uphill.

  2.0 — Cross Lake Louise Drive (Caution: traffic).

  2.3 — Junction (1725 m) with *Tramline* trail at km 4.1. Take it to the eastern end of the lower Lake Louise parking area 400 m away.

This trail provides a shorter but steeper approach than the *Tramline* trail to reach Lake Louise from the area of the village by the Bow River. The churning waters tumbling down the steep course of Louise Creek add variety to this outing.

This trail is not open to mountain biking because of its steep grades and the danger of collisions with hikers. The option for fat-tire bicyclists is the *Tramline* trail.

Especially when close to the creek with its boisterous bubbling, take care to make noise and look ahead as bears frequent this area, which is in a heavily used wildlife corridor.

# Kingfisher Lake

**Distance:** 0.2 km (0.1 mi) — Trans-Canada Highway to Kingfisher Lake
**Unmaintained trail:** 5—10 minutes one way
**Elevation gain:** 10 m (35 ft)
**Maximum elevation:** 1545 m (5070 ft)
**Trailhead:** A small grassy area on the east side of the Trans-Canada Highway, 1.1 km (0.7 mi) north of the bridge over the Bow River or 2.3 km (1.4 mi) south from where the on ramp from Lake Louise Village joins the highway. Parking is not recommended here; the easiest access is to take the barricaded emergency exit road from the RV section of the campground to the highway: a large wooden sign marks the trailhead just to the north on the opposite side of the highway. (**N.B.** Take care re. traffic when crossing the highway on foot.)

0.0 — Sign (elevation 1535 m). Climb a low ridge.
0.2 — Kingfisher Lake (1545 m).

Kingfisher Lake is a small, shallow body of water that holds no great interest, but it does provide for a brief diversion (most likely if staying at the campground). Although the lake is close to the Trans-Canada Highway, a low ridge keeps away most of the noise. The author has never seen a kingfisher here, but has sighted such species of waterfowl as common goldeneye, lesser scaup, and mallard.

**Kingfisher Lake.**

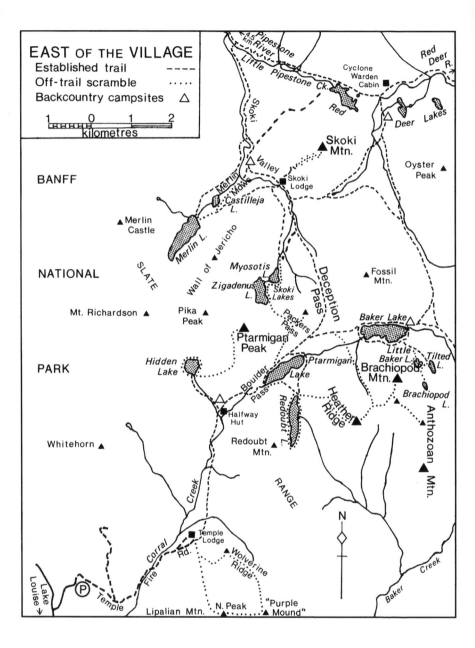

**EAST OF THE VILLAGE**

Established trail – – –
Off-trail scramble ·····
Backcountry campsites △

kilometres

Pipestone River

4.5 km

Little Pipestone Ck.

Red Deer R.

Cyclone Warden Cabin

Deer Lakes

Skoki Valley

Skoki Mtn.

Oyster Peak

BANFF

Merlin Maw

Castilleja L.

Skoki Lodge

Merlin Castle

Merlin L.

Wall of Jericho

NATIONAL

SLATE

Myosotis L.

Zigadenus L.

Skoki Lakes

Fossil Mtn.

Deception Pass

Mt. Richardson

Pika Peak

Packers Pass

Baker Lake

Ptarmigan Peak

PARK

Hidden Lake

Ptarmigan Lake

Little Baker L.

Tilted L.

Brachiopod Mtn.

Brachiopod L.

Boulder Pass

Halfway Hut

Redoubt L.

Heather Ridge

Anthozoan Mtn.

Whitehorn

Redoubt Mtn.

Creek

RANGE

N

Temple Lodge

Wolverine Ridge

Baker Creek

Lake Louise

P

Corral Rd.

Fire

Temple

Lipalian Mtn.

N. Peak

"Purple Mound"

# East of the Village

The rock formation known as Merlin Castle, above Merlin Lake (see p. 110).

# Boulder Pass

See photo p. 101 and second colour photo starting opposite p. 64.

**Distance:** 8.6 km (5.3 mi) — Fish Creek parking area to Boulder Pass
**Day hike/backpack:** 2.5—3 hours one way
**Elevation gain:** 655 m (2150 ft)
**Maximum elevation:** 2345 m (7690 ft)
**Trailhead:** The Fish Creek parking area, reached from the interchange on the Trans-Canada Highway by travelling 2.0 km (1.2 mi) up the Lake Louise Ski Area access road, passing the Bow Valley Parkway turnoff on the right. Turn right onto the gravel road and continue 1.1 km (0.7 mi) farther to the parking area. (There is no public access beyond this point.) **N.B.** The first 3.9 km of this trail is currently open to mountain biking. [There are plans to establish a bus service to transport hikers along this initial section.]

0.0 — Fish Creek parking area (elevation 1690 m). Head up the Temple Fire Road, which rises on a steady grade. Keep straight at the two intersections en route.

3.9 — End of the fire road (2010 m) beyond and above the ski area Temple Day Lodge, at a bridge at the far side of a ski run. (This is the starting point for the off-trail scramble *Lipalian Mountain and beyond*; see p. 119.) Turn right up short, steep incline, then bear left. Proceed north, climbing gradually.

6.5 — Reach open meadows and cross Corral Creek to west side.

7.0 — Cross footbridge over stream from Hidden Lake and keep left; Halfway Hut day-use shelter to right.

7.1 — Keep right at junction (2195 m) with *Hidden Lake* trail (see p. 100), which gives access to a backcountry campground in less than 100 m. Soon begin steady ascent.

8.6 — Boulder Pass (2345 m) just before the western end of Ptarmigan Lake.

The 3.9 km up the Temple Fire Road at the start of this outing do not make for an inspiring beginning. However, things improve once on the trail proper, with the prospect of visiting a classic subalpine valley and reaching the alpine zone at the end.

After travelling through coniferous forest (including subalpine larch trees) for about 2.5 km, break into open meadows with dazzling wildflowers in season. Here the sensation becomes one of spaciousness, albeit within a setting of rugged peaks.

The Halfway Hut day-use shelter can provide welcome respite in stormy conditions; other relief can be had in the adjacent outhouse. The name of the hut comes from back when it was the midway overnight stop on the trip to Skoki Lodge that began at Lake Louise Village. (See the fifth colour photo in the section starting opposite p. 64 for the setting of Halfway Hut in the meadows at the head of Corral Creek—the hut's roof shines as a small white area in the upper part of the image.)

The backcountry campground just off to the left on the *Hidden Lake* trail (see p. 100) at the km 7.1 junction can serve as a base to further explore the area. To get to Boulder Pass, keep right and climb more steeply past the large boulders that give the pass its name.

A marmot might be seen sunning itself on the rocks, though a careful search may be required as the grey coats of these animals allow them to blend in (their reddish

**Halfway Hut day-use shelter.**

tails can give them away).

Pikas are often observed in the vicinity of Boulder Pass as well. Being small, grey, and tailless, they too can be hard to spot, even when giving their high-pitched calls (which tend to be ventriloquistic). Look for pikas dashing about to feed on the wildflowers that provide sustenance for these energetic, non-hibernating small mammals. (For all their industriousness, pikas—which can only survive within a narrow temperature range—are showing signs of trouble in adapting to increases due to global warming.)

Boulder Pass overlooks Ptarmigan Lake, with views of the front ranges to the east. To the west rise Mt. Victoria, Mt. Temple, and several of the summits ringing the Valley of the Ten Peaks.

The white-tailed ptarmigan, the bird that gave its name to Ptarmigan Lake and Ptarmigan Peak (see p. 101), can often be seen in this area [see seventh page in section of colour photos beginning opposite p. 64].

# Hidden Lake

See fifth colour photo starting opposite p. 64.

**Distance:** 1.3 km (0.8 mi) — *Boulder Pass* trail to Hidden Lake
**Extension to day hike:** 30 minutes one way
**Elevation gain:** 85 m (280 ft)
**Maximum elevation:** 2280 m (7480 ft)
**Trailhead:** Km 7.1 on *Boulder Pass* trail (see previous two pages).

0.0 — Junction (elevation 2195 m). Keep left for Hidden Lake and pass the backcountry campground. Climb steadily.
1.3 — Hidden Lake (2280 m).

Hidden Lake, as its somewhat generic name suggests, lies in a side valley beneath high peaks of the Slate Range and is not readily visible. If on a day hike from the Fish Creek trailhead, choosing this as a destination rather than Boulder Pass would involve about the same distance but 60 m (200 ft) less elevation gain.

Hidden Lake is a natural choice for backpackers staying at the nearby campground who want to explore the area. An option once at the lake is to circumnavigate it on an off-trail jaunt.

The slopes above Hidden Lake represent one of the few areas in the Lake Louise wilderness where bighorn sheep are likely to be seen. Mountain goats may be observed in the cirque too. The meadows around Hidden Lake also support mule deer, able to move swiftly over rugged terrain. As a final wildlife note, this is grizzly bear habitat, so follow proper procedures.

Hidden Lake is the jumping-off point for the scramble up Ptarmigan Peak; see page opposite.

**Hiker above Hidden Lake, looking west.**

# Ptarmigan Peak

See photos p. 107 and p. 118.

**Distance:** 2.4 km (1.5 mi) — Hidden Lake to summit of Ptarmigan Peak
**Off-trail scramble:** 2.5—3 hours one way
**Elevation gain:** 779 m (2555 ft)
**Maximum elevation:** 3059 m (10,034 ft)
**Trailhead:** End of *Hidden Lake* trail (see page opposite).

0.0 — Hidden Lake (elevation 2280 m). Cross outflow creek at the south end of the lake and head easterly. Pass round the cliffs to the northeast and ascend the prominent south-facing gully. Veer right near the top of the gully to gain the summit ridge. Follow it east, negotiating a dip en route. (**N.B.** Exposure to a long fall on the north side.)

2.4 — Summit of Ptarmigan Peak (3059 m).

The ascent of this peak of the Slate Range leads to an elevation over the significant height of 3000 m, and the going is easy—even somewhat tedious on the scree—except for a short bit just before the top. **N.B.** This section exposes aspiring ascensionists to a major drop, so don't venture here if nervous about heights.

It was only in 1909 that the first climbers reached the top of Ptarmigan Peak, and not very many people go here even nowadays. The views, nevertheless, are superb, including all of Ptarmigan Lake below to the south, and a sea of peaks all round culminating in Mt. Assiniboine over 75 km away on the southern horizon.

**South from the slopes of Ptarmigan Peak over Boulder Pass and the west end of Ptarmigan Lake to Redoubt Mountain (r), Heather Ridge opposite it, and beyond.**

# Redoubt Lake

See second colour photo starting opposite p. 64.

**Distance:** 1.1 km (0.7 mi) — Boulder Pass to north end of Redoubt Lake
**Off-trail scramble:** 30 minutes one way
**Elevation gain:** 50 m (165 ft)
**Maximum elevation:** 2395 m (7855 ft)
**Trailhead:** Boulder Pass (see p. 98).

0.0 — Boulder Pass (elevation 2345 m) just before the western end of Ptarmigan Lake. Head along the south shore of Ptarmigan Lake [*Skoki Valley via Deception Pass* trail (see p. 104) goes along the north shore], picking a route over boulders.
0.5 — Veer uphill to right on faint path across an open slope.
1.1 — North end of Redoubt Lake (2395 m).

Redoubt Lake lies at the base of the east face of Redoubt Mountain, which was named by Alpine Club of Canada president A.O. Wheeler in 1908.

Once at the north end of the lake, it's feasible to make a circuit. There is a rough track along the west shore—a route shared with mountain goats, which may have moved up onto the east aspect of Redoubt Mountain in the face of human presence. To his surprise, the author has found forget-me-not still in bloom along this stretch in late September.

Travel back along the east shore of the lake is along the topmost of a series of ledges. This route stays above a cliffband overlooking a remote valley that feeds Baker Creek. Views to the south encompass Protection Mountain, Stuart Knob, and Pulsatilla Mountain.

To the west lies Heather Ridge, whose ascent can be made as per the description on the page opposite.

**Redoubt Lake and north to Fossil Mountain.**

# Heather Ridge

See photo p. 101.

**Distance:** 1.7 km (1.1 mi) — Redoubt Lake to summit of Heather Ridge
**Off-trail scramble:** 1—1.5 hour(s) one way
**Elevation gain:** 270 m (885 ft)
**Maximum elevation:** 2665 m (8740 ft)
**Trailhead:** End of *Redoubt Lake* trail (see page opposite).

0.0 — North end of Redoubt Lake (elevation 2395 m). Climb east to north end of Heather Ridge, then proceed southeast along ridge.
1.7 — Summit of Heather Ridge (2665 m).

Heather Ridge, as the name suggests, features wildflowers of the white, pink, and yellow mountain heather species. It also holds the bonus of a group of unusual spire-like rock pinnacles about one-third of the way along the crest.

A further highlight of Heather Ridge is the view it affords of the full length of Redoubt Lake. The furrowed east face of Redoubt Mountain rises above the lake; other conspicuous peaks visible from the summit include Mt. Temple and Hungabee Mountain to the southwest, and Mt. Richardson, Mt. Daly, and Mt. Balfour to the northwest.

A peregrine falcon with its typical pointed-wing silhouette might be glimpsed cruising over Heather Ridge.

It is possible to descend east from the summit to the saddle between it and Brachiopod Mountain, which connects with the description for the off-trail ascents of Brachiopod Mountain and Anthozoan Mountain (see p. 118).

**Pinnacles on Heather Ridge and northwest to Mt. Richardson (r) and Mt. Daly (l).**

# Skoki Valley via Deception Pass

**Distance:** 7.0 km (4.3 mi) — Boulder Pass to Merlin Meadows backcountry campground via Deception Pass
**Extension to day hike or backpack:** 1 hour one way to Deception Pass; an additional 1.5—2 hours one way to Merlin Meadows backcountry campground
**Elevation gain:** 134 m (440 ft) Boulder Pass to Deception Pass
**Elevation loss:** 374 m (1227 ft) Deception Pass to Merlin Meadows backcountry campground
**Maximum elevation:** 2474 m (8115 ft)
**Trailhead:** Boulder Pass (see p. 98).

0.0 — Boulder Pass (elevation 2345 m) just before the western end of Ptarmigan Lake. Take trail along north shore of Ptarmigan Lake.

0.6 — Keep straight at unmarked junction (2340 m) with *Skoki Valley via Packers Pass* trail (see p. 106) going off to left.

1.9 — Keep left at junction (2365 m) with *Baker Lake* trail (see p. 108). Begin steep climb.

2.4 — Deception Pass (2474 m). Descend north side on steady grade.

4.7 — Keep straight at unmarked junction (2205 m) with *Skoki Valley via Packers Pass* trail (see p. 106).

5.0 — Keep straight at a well-travelled horse trail veering off to the left after a creek crossing, in order to avoid mud and a narrow canyon.

5.3 — Keep left at junction (2195 m) with *Red Deer Lakes from Skoki Lodge* trail (see p. 109).

5.8 — Skoki Lodge (2165 m). Trail to Skoki Valley continues to rear of main building. *Merlin Lake* trail (see p. 110) starts from front of building and *Skoki Mountain* off-trail scramble (see p. 111) starts from rear of building.

7.0 — Merlin Meadows backcountry campground (2100 m).

**Glaciated northern aspect of Mt. Richardson from the Merlin Meadows backcountry campground in Skoki Valley.**

**Skoki Lodge.**

This trail from Boulder Pass along the north shore of Ptarmigan Lake and over Deception Pass is the usual approach to Skoki Valley. (The trip from the Fish Creek parking area to Deception Pass and back can be made in a long day, while pushing the pace can allow a trip to Skoki Lodge and return.)

A total of almost 16 km (about 10 mi) of travel from the Fish Creek trailhead sees arrival at the Merlin Meadows backcountry campground past Skoki Lodge. This can serve as an excellent base for exploring the vicinity. For example, two alternative connectors to the *Merlin Lake* trail start here (see p. 110).

It is even possible, sitting at a campsite picnic table, to observe the daily routine of mountain goats on the avalanche slopes and cliffs to the north.

The name of the valley is from a Native word meaning 'swamp' or 'marshy,' which is unflattering but accurate at least for the flat area beyond the campground. It also happens that one of the leaders of the first party of mountaineers to venture into the valley in 1911 was from Skokie, Illinois.

Information on Skoki Lodge, which has been declared a National Historic Site, is available on the website www.skokilodge.com and by toll-free phone at 1-800-258-7669.

# Skoki Valley via Packers Pass

**Distance:** 4.3 km (2.7 mi) — Ptarmigan Lake to *Skoki Valley via Deception Pass* trail
**Unofficial connector:** 30—40 minutes one way to Packers Pass; an additional 1—1.5 hour(s) one way to *Skoki Valley via Deception Pass* trail
**Elevation gain:** 140 m (460 ft) Ptarmigan Lake to Packers Pass
**Elevation loss:** 285 m (935 ft) Packers Pass to *Skoki Valley via Deception Pass* trail
**Maximum elevation:** 2480 m (8135 ft)
**Trailhead:** Km 0.6 on *Skoki Valley via Deception Pass* trail (see two previous pages).

0.0 — Unmarked junction (elevation 2340 m) on north shore of Ptarmigan Lake before the *Skoki Valley via Deception Pass* trail goes around a rocky point. Keep left up rocky incline on path that has become better defined in recent years but still becomes faint in open rocky area below the pass.

1.2 — Packers Pass (2480 m) A path continues north down toward Zigadenus Lake. The route descends a ramp beside the rockband east of and above this lake to Myosotis Lake. Continue along the south and east shores of Myosotis Lake, then descend the chimney in the rockband to the east, south of the waterfall from Myosotis Lake. **N.B.** This is the crux of this unofficial route, and although some informal improvements have been made it still involves hands-and-feet scrambling (climbing up is easier than descending). Once down on the flats below, keep right on an improving trail that leads through subalpine larches. (There is a trail on the far side of the creek but taking it requires a ford. It joins the *Merlin Lake* trail (see p. 110) at km 0.3.)

4.3 — Unmarked junction (2195 m) with *Skoki Valley via Deception Pass* trail (see two previous pages) at km 4.7.

**View from Packers Pass of Zigadenus Lake and the Wall of Jericho above.**

**West over Myosotis Lake to the glaciated eastern aspects of (l to r) Ptarmigan Peak and Pika Peak.**

This pass got its name because of its use by early packers. It fell out of favour as a trade route due to the tricky chimney in the rockband that dams Myosotis Lake. However, visiting Packers Pass, either as a destination itself or en route to Skoki Valley, is an interesting alternative to the main trail that goes over Deception Pass.

Bighorn sheep might be observed in the vicinity of Packers Pass. Arrival at the pass reveals the upper of the two Skoki Lakes: Zigadenus, a charming turquoise body of water with the unexpected backdrop of a glacier on neighbouring Ptarmigan and Pika peaks. The names of the two Skoki Lakes come from the scientific names for the genera of two wildflowers found in the area: white camas (*Zigadenus elegans*) and alpine forget-me-not (*Myosotis alpestris*).

An optional scramble is to the top of the knoll (2600 m) between Packers Pass and Deception Pass (see second photo in colour section beginning opposite p. 64).

Continuing beyond Packers Pass, the route descends toward Zigadenus Lake, with the first subalpine larches soon dotting the meadows. If it's a warm, calm day, it can be relaxing to listen to the sounds carrying from the waterfalls in the area.

Cairns generally mark the way, though they should not be uncritically exclusively relied upon for routefinding...in other words, as always, pay attention and take responsibility.

For the crux section, if backpacking and the choice is available, it may be easier to have one experienced person ferry the loads rather than having all members of the party squeeze through the tight spots with gear on their backs.

# Baker Lake

**Distance:** 2.6 km (1.6 mi) — Junction below Deception Pass (on south side) to backcountry campground at east end of Baker Lake
**Backpack:** 30—40 minutes one way
**Elevation loss:** 155 m (510 ft)
**Maximum elevation:** 2365 m (7755 ft)
**Trailhead:** Km 1.9 on *Skoki Valley via Deception Pass* trail (see p. 104).

0.0 — Junction (elevation 2365 m) below Deception Pass on its south side. Keep east for Baker Lake, descending gradually to the west end of the lake.

1.5 — Keep straight at junction at west end of Baker Lake with alternate trail that leads along its south shore and in 1.2 km joins *Tilted Lake and environs* trail (see p. 116) at km 0.5.

2.6 — East end of Baker Lake (2210 m) and backcountry campground.

The backcountry campground at the east end of Baker Lake is a popular base for day hikes in the area, such as to Tilted Lake and its environs (see p. 116) or up Brachiopod Mountain and Anthozoan Mountain (see p. 118).

Extended trips from Baker Lake can either go north toward Red Deer Lakes (see p. 115) or head south to descend the upper valley of Baker Creek to Wildflower Creek—below which there is no trail down Baker Creek—and then over Pulsatilla Pass (see p. 117).

The Baker Lake area is prime grizzly bear habitat, and moose also occur in the vicinity (see colour photo opposite p. 64).

**Baker Lake and Fossil Mountain from Brachiopod Mountain.**

# Red Deer Lakes from Skoki Lodge

**Distance:** 3.4 km (2.1 mi) — *Skoki Valley via Deception Pass* trail near Skoki Lodge
to Red Deer Lakes backcountry background
**Day hike or backpack:** 1—1.5 hour(s) one way
**Elevation gain:** 15 m (50 ft)
**Elevation loss:** 115 m (375 ft)
**Maximum elevation:** 2210 m (7250 ft)
**Trailhead:** Km 5.3 of *Skoki Valley via Deception Pass* trail (see p. 104).

0.0 — Sign (elevation 2195 m). Head east through gap between Fossil Mountain
and Skoki Mountain, sometimes referred to as 'Jones Pass' after pioneer packer
and guide Ken Jones.

0.6 — Keep straight (2210 m) where *Skoki Lodge—Baker Lake Shortcut* goes right.

2.7 — Keep left (2120 m) where *Red Deer Lakes from Baker Lake* trail comes in on
right.

3.1 — Keep right at junction for backcountry campground.

3.4 — Red Deer Lakes backcountry campground (2095 m).

The Red Deer Lakes are near the headwaters of the long Red Deer River that
flows through much of Alberta. The backcountry campground can serve as a stopover
on extended trips; options from here include taking the *Pipestone River from Red Deer
Lakes* trail (see p. 114) or connecting with Baker Lake (see p. 115).


# Skoki Lodge—Baker Lake Shortcut

**Distance:** 2.2 km (1.4 mi) — *Red Deer Lakes from Skoki Lodge* trail to *Red Deer
Lakes from Baker Lake* trail
**Connector:** 30 minutes one way
**Elevation gain:** 50 m (165 ft)
**Elevation loss:** 95 m (310 ft)
**Maximum elevation:** 2260 m (7415 ft)
**Trailhead:** Km 0.6 of *Red Deer Lakes from Skoki Lodge* trail (see above).

0.0 — Junction (elevation 2210 m); turn right.

1.2 — High point (2260 m). Proceed along base of ridge of Fossil Mountain.

2.2 — Join *Red Deer Lakes from Baker Lake* trail (2165 m) at km 3.5 (see p. 115).

This connector trail serves as a shortcut between the Skoki Lodge area and
Baker Lake, for example if travelling directly between the backcountry campgrounds at
Merlin Meadows and at the east end of Baker Lake.

# Merlin Lake

See photos on page opposite and on p. 97.

**Distance:** 3.1 km (1.9 mi) — Skoki Lodge to Merlin Lake
**Day hike and off-trail scramble:** 1—1.5 hour(s) one way
**Elevation gain:** 110 m (360 ft)
**Elevation loss:** 35 m (115 ft)
**Maximum elevation:** 2275 m (7460 ft)
**Trailhead:** Skoki Lodge, reached at km 5.8 on *Skoki Valley via Deception Pass* trail (see p. 104).

0.0 — Skoki Lodge (elevation 2165 m). Cross footbridge over the creek in front of the lodge and continue on narrow trail.

0.3 — Keep right at junction with alternative trail connecting with *Skoki Valley via Packers Pass* trail. Follow cairned route.

2.2 — Pass by south side of Castilleja Lake (a faint path leads down to the lake). Climb steeply following cairns.

2.9 — High point (2275 m) on ridge above Merlin Lake.

3.1 — East end of Merlin Lake (2240 m).

Lawrence Grassi, a dedicated trail builder best-known for his work in the Lake O'Hara region of Yoho National Park (just west of Lake Louise), built the first section of this trail. The trail passes Castilleja Lake, named like the Skoki Lakes after a wildflower, in this case paintbrush (*Castilleja* genus).

Then this outing becomes a scramble up through a gap on the south side of a cliffband to reach Merlin Lake. The effort is well worthwhile: the lake has a wild, remote character. An intriguing aspect of Merlin Lake is that its drainage is not by way of a waterfall, but via a subterranean river that issues forth at the base of the cliffband.

Overlooking the lake is the formation known as Merlin Castle, a cluster of tall rock spires. Incidentally, the name of these features comes from the fancied resemblance of these pinnacles to the abode of the famous magician.

An alternative approach to Merlin Lake begins at the Merlin Meadows backcountry campground and heads west across the meadows on a wet, ambiguous route. A rough trail up an incline beside a waterfall leads to Castilleja Lake. A path along its south shore suddenly turns away from the water and shortly joins the trail described above at km 2.2.

It's a worthwhile exploratory trip to navigate cross-country from the east end of Merlin Lake to Merlin Ridge, the high crest at the head of the valley. (There are no glaciers on this ridge, despite the possible indication on some maps.) On a classic fall day in September, 1991, the author made this journey in a party led from Skoki Lodge by renowned mountain guide Ken Jones (now deceased). As Ken put it, "You don't necessarily get the best views from the highest peaks:" a saying verified in the panoramic vistas from Merlin Ridge.

An optional exit from Merlin Lake is possible via an old horse trail that starts at the northeast corner of Merlin Lake and travels along the north side of the valley. At its end awaits a ford of the creek—or possibly a crossing on a log bridge lower down—to the Merlin Meadows backcountry campground, reached in about 2.6 km.

# Skoki Mountain

See photo p. 114.

**Distance:** 1.6 km (1.0 mi) — Skoki Lodge to summit of Skoki Mountain
**Off-trail scramble:** 1.5—2 hours one way
**Elevation gain:** 532 m (1745 ft)
**Maximum elevation:** 2697 m (8846 ft)
**Trailhead:** Skoki Lodge, reached at km 5.8 on *Skoki Valley via Deception Pass* trail (see p. 104).

0.0 — Skoki Lodge (elevation 2165 m). Pick up this trail behind the lodge, probably near the outhouse (not to be confused with the *Skoki Valley via Deception Pass* trail continuing to Merlin Meadows). Climb through forest, then above treelimit zigzag up the western aspect on a vague path more easily seen on the descent.
1.6 — Summit of Skoki Mountain (2697 m).

Skoki Mountain isn't a spectacular peak, and getting to its top is basically a scree slog, but it does grant a superb overview of the area (again confirming Ken Jones' observation near the bottom of the page opposite).

From the summit, Mt. Douglas and Mt. St. Bride stand prominent to the east, while to the west lies intriguing Merlin Valley with the glaciated north face of Mt. Richardson at its head.

Skoki Mountain also allows views of the routes into this area via Deception Pass and Packers Pass, as well as of the Skoki Lakes. Above those two turquoise bodies of water that share the name of this feature rise the cliffs of the east faces of Ptarmigan Peak and Pika Peak, which are also host to a surprisingly large glacier.

Skoki Mountain stands north of Fossil Mountain, which can be ascended and traversed from either the valley below Skoki Mountain to the south or (more readily) from Deception Pass.

**Merlin Lake, Ridge, and Castle (on right), and Castilleja Lake from Skoki Mountain.**

111

# Red Deer Lakes from Skoki Valley

See photo on page opposite.

**Distance:** 5.2 km (3.2 mi) — Skoki Valley to Red Deer Lakes backcountry campground
**Connector:** 1.5—2 hours one way
**Elevation gain:** 70 m (230 ft)
**Elevation loss:** 75 m (245 ft)
**Maximum elevation:** 2165 m (7100 ft)
**Trailhead:** Merlin Meadows backcountry campground at end of *Skoki Valley via Deception Pass* trail (see p. 104).

0.0 — Merlin Meadows backcountry campground (elevation 2100 m) in Skoki Valley. Take trail heading north from campground.

0.2 — Keep right at junction (2095 m) with *Little Pipestone Creek from Skoki Valley* trail (see page opposite).

3.1 — Horse corral. Trail becomes braided; keep northeast and cross nascent Little Pipestone Creek just below outlet from the largest of the Red Deer Lakes.

3.6 — Keep right at junction (2095 m) with start of *Pipestone River from Red Deer Lakes* trail (see p. 114).

4.0 — Keep straight at junction with faint trail that veers off to southeast.

4.7 — Turn right at junction with trail down the Red Deer River (see the author's **Backcountry Banff**, Luminous Compositions). Cyclone warden cabin 400 m east.

5.2 — Red Deer Lakes backcountry campground (2095 m). See p. 109 for access here from Skoki Lodge, or p. 115 for access from Baker Lake.

This trail travels mostly through forest until it reaches the vast open meadows in which lie the Red Deer Lakes, so it is mainly of use to connect the two backcountry campgrounds.

The going gets vague near the lakes themselves due to a proliferation of trails, but by this point the terrain allows for easier navigation.

# Little Pipestone Creek from Skoki Valley

See photo p. 114.

**Distance:** 3.0 km (1.9 mi) — Skoki Valley to Little Pipestone Creek
**Connector:** 1 hour one way
**Elevation loss:** 145 m (475 ft)
**Maximum elevation:** 2095 m (6870 ft)
**Trailhead:** Km 0.2 of *Red Deer Lakes from Skoki Valley* trail (see page opposite).

0.0 — Junction (elevation 2095 m). Keep straight, heading down drainage. The going can be vague here.

2.7 — Possibly encounter an old black-and-white sign indicating that the trail veers sharply to the right. Ford or jump across Little Pipestone Creek and head straight east across grassy meadows.

3.0 — Unsigned junction (1950 m) with *Pipestone River from Red Deer Lakes* trail at approximately km 2.4 (see next page).

This seldom-used trail comes into use for those heading to the Pipestone River from Skoki Valley. A highlight is the view of Molar Mountain with its twin peaks, making apparent the origin of its name. Wolves may be heard or even seen in this relatively remote region.

**Mt. Douglas from Red Deer Lakes.**

# Pipestone River from Red Deer Lakes

**Distance:** 7.2 km (4.5 mi) — Red Deer Lakes to Pipestone River
**Backpack:** 2—2.5 hours one way
**Elevation loss:** 285 m (935 ft)
**Maximum elevation:** 2095 m (6870 ft)
**Trailhead:** Km 3.6 on *Red Deer Lakes from Skoki Valley* trail (see p. 112).

0.0 — Junction (elevation 2095 m). Head northwesterly on trail that stays north of Little Pipestone Creek.

2.4 — Unmarked junction (1950 m) with *Little Pipestone Creek from Skoki Valley* trail. Keep right and pass section of open meadow beside the creek.

2.7 — Keep right at junction. **Important:** If doing this trail in the opposite direction, keep left at this junction, whether headed for the Red Deer Lakes or Skoki Valley (contrary to possible signed indications) since going straight leads into marshy terrain that can be negotiated on horseback but is soggy and confusing on foot.

7.2 — Pipestone River (1810 m) at Little Pipestone warden cabin. The *Lower Pipestone Valley* trail (see p. 122) heads downstream from here, while fording the river [**N.B.** Caution] leads into territory covered in the author's **Backcountry Banff** (Luminous Compositions).

A highlight of this trail is the view of Mt. Hector as heading west through the open meadows near and below the largest of the Red Deer Lakes. This is the only trail in the Lake Louise area from which the extensive glacier on the north slopes of Mt. Hector can be seen. There is also an expansive view to the east, including the usually snow-capped summit of Mt. Douglas—named in honour of Scottish botanist David Douglas (for whom the Douglas fir tree is also named).

**Northeast down the valley of Little Pipestone Creek from the summit of Skoki Mountain, with the landmarks of Mt. Hector (left of centre) and Molar Mountain (centre).**

# Red Deer Lakes from Baker Lake

**Distance:** 5.1 km (3.2 mi) — Baker Lake to *Red Deer Lakes from Skoki Lodge* trail
**Backpack:** 1.5 hours one way
**Elevation loss:** 90 m (295 ft)
**Maximum elevation:** 2210 m (7250 ft)
**Trailhead:** Backcountry campground at east end of Baker Lake; see *Baker Lake* trail description, p. 108.

0.0 — Backcountry campground at east end of Baker Lake (elevation 2210 m). Head northeast on trail that runs parallel to and slightly higher than another trail used mainly by horse parties.

0.7 — Keep left at junction with connector that runs south 700 m to join *Upper Baker Creek and Pulsatilla Pass* trail (see p. 117) at km 0.8.

3.5 — Keep straight at junction (2165 m) with *Skoki Lodge—Baker Lake Shortcut* trail.

5.1 — Junction (2120 m) with *Red Deer Lakes from Skoki Lodge* trail at km 2.7 (see p. 109).

This trail connects the backcountry campgrounds at Baker Lake and Red Deer Lakes. It passes through the open meadows between Fossil Mountain and Oyster Peak (referred to by some as 'Cotton Grass Pass'), which offer fine views. They also represent perfect territory for northern harriers...the author once watched a rusty brown female quartering tirelessly over the flats, searching for rodent prey with her long yellow legs ready to grab a meal.

Then the trail drops into the wooded drainage between Oyster Peak and Fossil Mountain, whose creek originates at Oyster Lake in the basin to the east.

This trail, in conjunction with the *Baker Lake* trail (see p. 108) and *Skoki Lodge—Baker Lake Shortcut* trail (see p. 109), can be used to approach or exit Skoki Valley from the Lake Louise side without having to climb over Deception Pass. Of course, the distance is greater, by 4.9 km.

# Tilted Lake and environs

**Distance:** 1.5 km (0.9 mi) — East end of Baker Lake to Tilted Lake
**Day hike** (from Baker Lake backcountry campground): 30 minutes one way
**Elevation gain:** 25 m (80 ft)
**Elevation loss:** 15 m (50 ft)
**Maximum elevation:** 2235 m (7330 ft)
**Trailhead:** Backcountry campground at east end of Baker Lake; see *Baker Lake* trail description, p. 108.

0.0 — Baker Lake backcountry campground (elevation 2210 m). Head south, cross the outlet stream, and follow the south shore of the lake.
0.5 — Keep left at junction with alternate trail that goes around west end of the lake and connects with *Baker Lake* trail (see p. 108) in 1.2 km. Climb open slope to go into subalpine forest.
1.1 — High point (2235 m).
1.5 — Tilted Lake (2220 m).

The established trail from the south shore of Baker Lake leads to Tilted Lake, not to Little Baker Lake as may be indicated on some maps. Little Baker Lake lies some 300 m to the west of Tilted Lake via cross-country travel. One off-trail option on leaving Little Baker Lake is to descend beside a small stream running north through a narrow gorge from its northwest end.

Nearby Brachiopod Lake, below the mountain of the same name, hardly deserves to be recorded by cartographers: it is tiny, and was surrounded by mud on one visit by the author.

The area south of Baker Lake is frequented by grizzly bears, as is apparent from their many diggings. Moose also occur in the vicinity.

**American dipper.**

# Upper Baker Creek and Pulsatilla Pass

**Distance:** 12.5 km (7.8 mi) — East end of Baker Lake to Pulsatilla Pass
**Backpack:** 4—5 hours one way
**Elevation loss:** 380 m (1245 ft) Baker Lake to Wildflower Creek
**Elevation gain:** 525 m (1720 ft) Wildflower Creek to Pulsatilla Pass
**Maximum elevation:** 2355 m (7725 ft)
**Trailhead:** Backcountry campground at east end of Baker Lake; see *Baker Lake* trail description, p. 108.

0.0 — Baker Lake backcountry campground (elevation 2210 m). Head southeast toward vast open meadows.

0.8 — Keep right at junction with connector that runs north 700 m to join *Red Deer Lakes from Baker Lake* trail (see p. 115) at km 0.7.

2.3 — Leave extensive open meadows. The trail descends steeply through forest on the east side of the creek.

4.5 — Open meadow in which the way becomes ambiguous.

6.1 — Cross footbridge to Wildflower Creek backcountry campground (1830 m). To continue to Pulsatilla Pass, take steep trail uphill to east on south side of creek.

7.0 — Cross to north side of Wildflower Creek.

10.6 — Go either way at the junction: either on the highline that stays above Pulsatilla Lake or on the trail that drops slightly to go along the east side of the lake.

12.5 — Pulsatilla Pass (2355 m). For description of the trail beyond down Johnston Creek, see the author's **Backcountry Banff** (Luminous Compositions).

In the interests of wildlife, the former trail up Baker Creek from the Bow Valley Parkway is no longer maintained, but it is still possible to visit the upper part of the valley and to continue to Pulsatilla Pass via this trail from Baker Lake. The open meadows lying between Brachiopod Mountain and Tilted Mountain allow expansive views before diving into forest on the plunge toward Wildflower Creek.

Heading up Wildflower Creek leads into a remote valley with rugged beauty: its isolation suggested by the sighting the author once had of a wolverine. American dippers can also be observed in this high mountain stream, typical of the summer habitat of these small, plump, grey birds. They look nondescript but are fascinating. Dippers have oil producing glands that enable them to keep their feathers waterproof, and have ridges on the bases of their toes to grip on the rocky bottoms of rushing streams as they forage for invertebrates and tiny fish.

Dippers use their wings for propulsion as they swim about. Their habit while perched on rocks of frequently bending their legs in a bobbing motion gave rise to the name of these birds. They were favourites of naturalist/philosopher John Muir, who enjoyed the clear, melodious song dippers give in all seasons. Dipper nests are domes of moss built in a location protected from terrestrial predators, often on a canyon wall and even in the spray from a waterfall.

The trail gains the zone of subalpine larches near the basin holding surprisingly big Pulsatilla Lake, then heads up a final incline to Pulsatilla Pass.

# Brachiopod Mountain and Anthozoan Mountain

See photo p. 108.

**Distances:** Variable, depending on routes taken
**Off-trail scrambles:** Times variable
**Elevation gains:** Variable
**Maximum elevation:** 2660 m (8725 ft) Brachiopod Mountain
2660 m (8725 ft) North peak of Anthozoan Mountain
**Trailheads:** Variable.

Ascents of Brachiopod Mountain and Anthozoan Mountain provide interesting scrambles in the Baker Lake area. Distance, time, and elevation gain vary with the off-trail approach: whether from the backcountry campground at the east end of Baker Lake, from below Deception Pass, or from Heather Ridge by descending east.

However arrived at, the usual starting point for these scrambles is the saddle between Heather Ridge and Brachiopod Mountain. A steep path created by mountain goats (one of many such paths in this seldom-visited area; keep an eye out for the stocky white animals themselves) leads up a scree slope on the western aspect of Brachiopod Mountain to a dip in the summit ridge. To reach the summit from here, contour along the west face, then use some hands-and-feet moves to negotiate the steep but relatively solid grey limestone.

Returning to the dip in the ridge, it is possible to continue south over an easy subsidiary peak and descend to the saddle between Brachiopod Mountain and Anthozoan Mountain. The northwest scree slope of Anthozoan Mountain leads to a large cairn on the north peak. Although not the highest point on the mountain, it affords rewarding views over the environs of Baker Creek. Reaching the true summit (the south peak) calls for a traverse of over a kilometre along a steep, broken ridgecrest.

Even in late summer, snowpatches may provide the opportunity to do some glissading on descending from these two satisfying scrambles.

**North from the north peak of Anthozoan Mountain to Brachiopod Mountain in right foreground, and (l to r) Mt. Richardson, Ptarmigan Peak, and Fossil Mountain.**

# Lipalian Mountain and beyond

**Distance:** 2.7 km (1.7 mi) — End of Temple Fire Road to summit of Lipalian
Mountain
**Off-trail scramble:** 1.5—2 hours one way to summit of Lipalian Mountain
**Elevation gain:** 705 m (2310 ft)
**Maximum elevation:** 2715 m (8905 ft)
**Trailhead:** End of Temple Fire Road at km 3.9 on *Boulder Pass* trail (see p. 98).

0.0 — End of Temple Fire Road (elevation 2010 m). Head south up steep ski lift
maintenance track (*Boulder Pass* trail goes off to the left).
1.1 — Upper terminal on ski lift. Continue south on off-trail route onto northwest ridge of Lipalian Mountain. Initially on slippery slopes of splintered shale,
the rock changes to more pleasurable conglomerate near the crest.
2.3 — North peak of Lipalian Mountain. Head south over easy ground of summit
ridge.
2.7 — Summit of Lipalian Mountain (2715 m).

Lipalian Mountain, above Lake Louise Village on the east side of the Bow
Valley, has an obscure name and is eclipsed by the more dramatic peaks of the continental divide. It is nevertheless worth a visit, and presents additional options.

Lipalian Mountain's moniker has geological origins, in keeping with other
mountains in the Slate Range such as Anthozoan, Brachiopod, and Fossil. Eminent
paleontologist Dr. Charles Walcott gave these names around 1900.

The summit of Lipalian Mountain grants an impressive vista extending from
Mt. Assiniboine in the south to Mt. Forbes in the north, thus taking in the two highest
peaks in Banff National Park (both Matterhorn-shaped). Hidden Lake is not hidden
from here; neither are other lakes in the vicinity including Louise, Moraine, Island,
Kingfisher, Mud, Herbert, and Hector.

Return the same way, or as an alternative head east from the north peak,
down to a saddle and up to 'Purple Mound' (unofficial name due to rock colour). Finish this outing with a leisurely perambulation along 'Wolverine Ridge' below to the
north. Then hop and slide west down scree and through a few trees to pick up a ski-
hill access track that leads down to the Temple Fire Road.

**Vista including Mt.
Victoria, Fairview
Mountain, and Lake
Louise from summit
of Lipalian Mountain.**

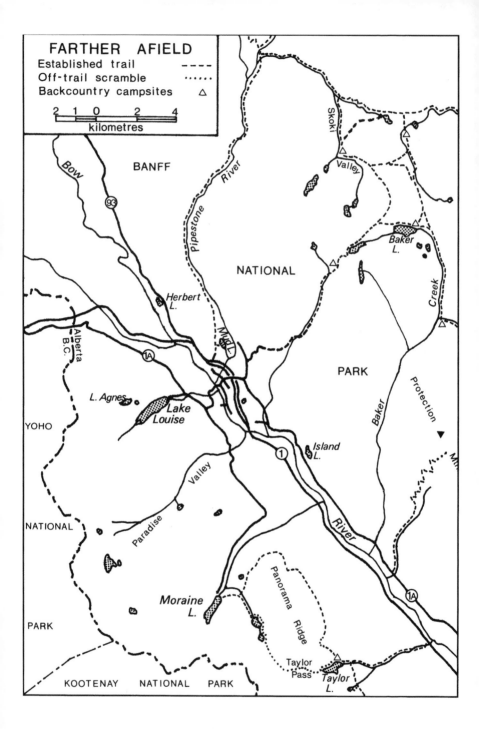

FARTHER AFIELD

Established trail
Off-trail scramble
Backcountry campsites △

2 1 0 2 4
kilometres

BANFF

Bow

93

Pipestone River

Skoki

Valley

NATIONAL

Baker
L.

Creek

Herbert
L.

Mud L.

PARK

Alberta
B.C.

1A

Baker

Protection

L. Agnes

Lake
Louise

YOHO

Island
L.

Valley

NATIONAL

Paradise

River

1

PARK

Moraine
L.

Panorama Ridge

1A

Taylor
Pass

Taylor
L.

KOOTENAY   NATIONAL   PARK

# Farther Afield

**East over Taylor Lake from south shore; (l to r) Protection Mountain and Castle Mountain on skyline.**

# Lower Pipestone Valley

See photo p. 49.

**Distance:** 18.0 km (11.2 mi) — Lake Louise Village area to Little Pipestone warden cabin
**Backpack:** 4—4.5 hours one way
**Elevation gain:** 255 m (835 ft)
**Maximum elevation:** 1810 m (5935 ft)
**Trailhead:** Turn north off the Trans-Canada Highway onto Slate Road, 1.0 km (0.6 mi) west of the Lake Louise overpass. Keep left at the first junction, then turn right at the top of the hill. The parking area is on the right. **N.B.** The first 7.0 km of this trail is open to mountain biking.

0.0 — Trail shelter (elevation 1555 m). Head straight at first, then turn hard left uphill on gravel road.

0.4 — Turn left off road onto trail (there may be signs for number 1 cross-country ski trail: keep on this trail until km 7.0).

0.9 — Keep straight at junction with trail to Mud Lake, 600 m to the right.

7.0 — Keep straight at junction with cross-country ski trail that goes off to the left. The designated mountain biking trail ends here.

14.5 — Cross to east bank of Pipestone River. **N.B.** This is a hazardous ford, especially in high water.

17.5 — Ford Little Pipestone Creek (usually easy).

18.0 — Little Pipestone warden cabin (1810 m). To continue from here, either turn up the *Pipestone River from Red Deer Lakes* trail (see p. 114) for access to the Skoki Valley area or ford the river again [N.B. Caution] into territory covered in the author's companion guidebook **Backcountry Banff** (Luminous Compositions).

Native people utilized deposits of a particular type of shale found along the banks of this river to fashion pipe bowls and other artifacts. Hiking or backpacking up the lower part of the Pipestone Valley is not particularly inspiring, either in terms of the views or of the state of the trail itself, which can be very muddy. A redeeming feature of this outing is the variety of wildflowers that can be found.

**East over the valley of the Pipestone River from the summit of Mt. St. Piran.**

# Protection Mountain Minesite

**Distance:** 6.0 km (3.7 mi) — Bow Valley Parkway to abandoned mining camp on the western aspect of Protection Mountain
**Unofficial trail:** 3—3.5 hours one way
**Elevation gain:** 865 m (2835 ft)
**Maximum elevation:** 2350 m (7710 ft)
**Trailhead:** Parking area on the west side of the Bow Valley Parkway (Hwy. 1A), 1.6 km (1.0 mi) south of the highway bridge over Baker Creek and 1.5 km (0.9 mi) north of the Protection Mountain campground entrance. The distance southeast on the Bow Valley Parkway (Hwy. 1A) from its northern end at the Lake Louise ski area access road is 14.1 km (8.7 mi); northwest from Castle Junction the distance is 12.4 km (7.7 mi).

0.0 — Bow Valley Parkway (elevation 1485 m). From the east side of the road, pick up a path along the north side of the creek.
0.1 — Keep straight at a small footbridge across the creek to its south side. The trail climbs gradually at first (and is vague in places), then switchbacks steeply up.
6.0 — Abandoned mining camp buildings (2350 m).

This little-known but highly recommended trail climbs steeply to reach the remains of a mining camp above treelimit on the western slopes of Protection Mountain. The high location grants a spectacular view west over the Bow Valley to the peaks of the continental divide, a vista that may have been of some solace to the miners when relaxing from their toils.

Those involved in this operation, which dates from the late 1800s, put a lot of energy into establishing the well-designed switchbacks up to the minesite. There are some mining tunnels in the vicinity. (**N.B.** Exercise caution if entering any of them.)

It is possible to continue up to the summit ridge of Protection Mountain, and even to do a long ridgewalk that exits at Castle Junction: see the author's **Ridgewalks in the Canadian Rockies** (Luminous Compositions).

**Mts. Temple, Lefroy, and Victoria (l to r) in view west from entrance to horizontal mine shaft on Protection Mountain.**

# Taylor Lake from Trans-Canada Highway

See photo p. 121.

**Distance:** 6.3 km (3.9 mi) — Trans-Canada Highway to Taylor Lake
**Day hike or backpack:** 2—3 hours one way
**Elevation gain:** 595 m (1950 ft)
**Maximum elevation:** 2065 m (6775 ft)
**Trailhead:** Taylor Creek picnic area on the southwest side of the Trans-Canada Highway, 17.0 km (10.5 mi) southeast from the Lake Louise interchange or 8.0 km (5.0 mi) northwest of Castle Junction. **N.B.** There is a no left turn sign from the northbound lane of the highway, heading toward Lake Louise.

0.0 — Footbridge at west end of parking area (elevation 1470 m). Cross Taylor Creek and head upstream along south side.
1.0 — Cross footbridge to north side of Taylor Creek and begin steady climb on long switchbacks.
6.0 — Keep straight at junction with trail to O'Brien Lake and on to Boom Lake trail to left (see author's **Backcountry Banff**, Luminous Compositions).
6.3 —East end of Taylor Lake (2065 m) and backcountry campground.

This trail rises steadily through forest, and is perhaps most often used in fall when hikers wishing to see golden subalpine larches come here—to avoid the crowds at places such as Larch Valley—and head up to the valley just 500 m from the end of this trail. (See *Taylor Lake from Valley of the Ten Peaks*, p. 84.)

Another option is to use the Taylor Lake backcountry campground as a base for forays to Taylor Pass (see next page) and O'Brien Lake just 2.1 km away (see **Backcountry Banff** by the author). Of course, it could also serve as a stopover in an extended trip, e.g., south via unmaintained trail to the Boom Lake trail and beyond (again, see **Backcountry Banff**).

**West from Taylor Lake toward Taylor Pass between the ridge of Mt. Bell on the left and the base of the south end of Panorama Ridge on the right.**

# Taylor Pass

See photos on page opposite, on p. 82, and on seventh page of colour photos starting opposite p. 64.

**Distance:** 3.0 km (1.9 mi) — Taylor Lake over Taylor Pass to *Consolation Pass* route
**Off-trail scramble:** 2.5—3 hours one way
**Elevation gain:** 365 m (1195 ft) Taylor Lake to Taylor Pass
**Elevation loss:** 165 m (540 ft) Taylor Pass to *Consolation Pass* route
**Maximum elevation:** 2430 m (7970 ft)
**Trailhead:** Backcountry campground at east end of Taylor Lake (see page opposite).

0.0 — East end of Taylor Lake (elevation 2065 m). Proceed beyond backcountry campground on rough trail along the north side of lake.
1.1 — West end of Taylor Lake. Pass beneath waterfall and climb up gully on its south side, then head up steep slopes toward the obvious notch.
2.5 — Taylor Pass (2430 m).
3.0 — Point (about 2265 m) at which this route joins the *Consolation Pass* route (see p. 86) at approximately km 3.0.

This ambitious off-trail scramble leads to the saddle between Panorama Ridge and a spur of Mt. Bell, whose northern cliffs brood over Taylor Lake. It involves pushing through overgrown sections of trail, balancing along a narrow, exposed traverse, and forging up steep slopes that may have late-lying snow patches. (**N.B.** Although it does not require glacier travel, as suggested on some maps, an ice axe is still recommended.)

From Taylor Pass, there are views southeast down the Bow Valley to Castle Mountain and east across to Protection Mountain. Descending the west side of the pass into Consolation Valley enables a link with Moraine Lake via the *Consolation Pass* route (see p. 86) and the trails below it (see p. 85 and pages 81-82).

**The author at Taylor Pass, looking east to the Bow Valley.**

# Index

# Notes

# The Author

**The author and his wife Jane on the summit of Saddle Mountain in 2003, with view to the north including Mt. Hector (left) and the peaks of the Slate Range (right).**

Mike Potter first hiked in the Lake Louise region in 1970 and knows it intimately, from majestic mountains to brilliant butterflies.

From 1983 to 1996, Mike worked as an interpretive naturalist with Parks Canada, leading guided walks and presenting evening programs to park visitors. During his Parks career, he was based in Lake Louise for the summers of 1986 and 1989.

Mike, a writer and photographer with numerous freelance articles, established Luminous Compositions as a book publishing business in 1990.

Mike is the author of six other titles on the Canadian Rockies, including the companion to this volume: **Backcountry Banff** (revised edition 2001), which covers all of Banff National Park outside the Lake Louise area. His other books include **Central Rockies Wildflowers** (revised edition 2005), **Ridgewalks in the Canadian Rockies** (revised edition 2003), **White Wilderness: The Canadian Rockies in Winter** (2001), **Fire Lookout Hikes in the Canadian Rockies** (1998), and **Central Rockies Placenames** (1997).

Mike's business Luminous Compositions is the publisher of two other books: **Central Rockies Mammals** by John Marriott (revised edition 2005) and **Columbia Valley Guide** by Denise Lemaster (1997).

Mike savours the outdoors, finding inspiration there as did J. Norman Collie, who wrote in 1912: "the wanderer amongst the great mountains can sleep peacefully and dream of the snows and mighty woods, of the rushing rivers, and the clear lakes reflecting the white clouds, and the rock peaks, and can feel with far more certainty than most that all's well with the world."